THE HIGH THAT COULDN'T LAST

Teens and Drugs, From Experimentation to Addiction

By Youth Communication

Edited by Virginia Vitzthum

YOUTH COMMUNICATION

True Stories by Teens

THE HIGH THAT COULDN'T LAST

EXECUTIVE EDITORS
Keith Hefner and Laura Longhine

CONTRIBUTING EDITORS
Nora McCarthy, Rachel Blustain, Al Desetta, Andrea Estepa, Sheila Feeney, Clarence Haynes, Katia Hetter, Kendra Hurley, and Philip Kay

LAYOUT & DESIGN
Efrain Reyes, Jr. and Jeff Faerber

COVER ART
James Faber / YC Art Dept.

ISBN 978-1-935552-22-2

Second, Expanded Edition

Printed in the United States of America

Youth Communication ®
New York, NY
www.youthcomm.org

Catalog Item #YD06-1

Table of Contents

Contents

Contents

Numbing Out the Past

> Popping pills helps Miguel forget his seemingly endless
> pain, to the point where he no longer feels able to face
> his problems without drugs.

Busted!

> The writer describes the nightmare of being arrested for
> selling drugs.

My Coke Phase

> A friend introduces the writer to cocaine. Within two
> months she's doing drugs several times a day. A year
> after quitting she's still suffering the consequences.

> An explaination of the kinds of drug treatment
> available and where to find more information.

FICTION SPECIAL: Lost and Found

Using the Book

Introduction

It's easy to forget how often people use drugs, legal or illegal, to help them deal with life. Substance abuse is all around us. In the first story in this book, Antwaun Garcia writes, "When I was a kid, I noticed how family members picked up a cigarette whenever they felt stress or got mad." He describes how soon after that, he started to push down his own anxiety and sadness, first with cigarettes, then Bacardi, then weed.

That's the thing with drugs. Most people know they're not good for you, but they do make you feel better—right away. "I loved that being high or drunk made me forget everything that worried me," says the author of "Hooked on Heroin." Writing about his first hit of weed, Ashunte Hunt says he felt, "A calming, mellow sensation that I'd never felt in my life—I wanted to feel that way all the time."

When M. Lopez took ecstasy, she writes, "I felt flooded with compassion and empathy for those around me, and 110 percent more sensitive in every particle of my body." The writer of "My Coke Phase" remembers her first night taking cocaine: "I was a lot more sociable that night than I usually am. I didn't feel shy at all."

It's hard to "Just Say No" to such immediate relief, pleasure, and confidence.

But as the writers here discover, the high never lasts. The medicine becomes a poison. For some, the downside appears right away. X. Reyes found that marijuana gave him flashbacks of his adopted mother's abuse, and he gave it up after "seven weeks of hell." The anonymous writer of "If You Trip, You Might Fall," writes of terrifying hallucinations and feeling out of control. "Busted" describes the fear and loneliness of spending six months in jail on a drug charge.

Most of the stories are about a slightly slower decline into addiction. The writer of "My Coke Phase" describes how her use crept up: "At first I was doing just three or four lines a week, usually before I went out with my friends or after I had a bad day. After a couple of weeks, I started doing two lines, three times a day (about half a gram)." Soon she's doing several grams a day, stops going to high school, and has destroyed the inside of her nose. The writers here lose friends, family, jobs, and their freedom on their way to "rock bottom."

All the writers in this book share the courage and self-knowledge to face what drugs are doing to them. As the writer of "How to Get to LaLa Land," puts it, "After [you come down], you feel even sadder than before. And you realize that being high, and numb to your pain, can be dangerous, too." The author of "Smoke and Mirrors" realizes that "When I wasn't high, it was harder for me to concentrate, and sometimes I wouldn't feel like myself." Many of the writers report losing their interest in school and other things that used to give them pleasure, feeling separate from everyone, and above all, being controlled by their addictions.

Most of these teen writers get clean—or at least cleaner. Often the support of a loved one gives them the strength to recover. Many describe replacing the drug with art-making or exercising or helping someone. M. Lopez weaned herself from ecstasy this way: "I started to get lots of sleep and good eats, surrounded myself with loads of chipper, upbeat friends." Several writers describe stays in rehab facilities.

Readers who've gotten too deeply into an addictive substance will recognize their own struggles in these stories. Those who haven't will see a true portrait of why drugs are so seductive and how hard they are to give up. And everyone will see the specific steps these brave writers took to get their lives and their minds back.

In the following stories, names have been changed: *Last Man Standing, Hooked on Heroin, Losing My Life to Drugs, Interviews With Dealers, My So-Called Holidays,* and *My Coke Phase.*

Kaisha Jones

Clean and Kind of Sober

By Antwaun Garcia

When I was a kid, I noticed how family members picked up a cigarette whenever they felt stress or got mad. My mom would hand me her bogie (cigarette) and tell me to flush it down the toilet. One day, when I was 9, I closed the bathroom door and smoked it.

I figured that if my parents saw me smoking they'd laugh, like parents do when they watch a little girl walk in high heels impersonating her mother. But soon I used cigarettes the same way my parents did—to feel better.

When I was 10, my life got stressful. My friend Ricky died in a fire, and I went into foster care, moving from Manhattan to my aunt's house in Queens, NY, because my mom was using drugs.

When I couldn't read a book my aunt gave me, or thought about how my dad used to hit my mom, or wondered what my mom was doing on the streets, I couldn't wait to smoke a cigarette. Sometimes I even sneaked a little alcohol. At family parties my grandma had let us try it, and it made me feel loose.

Then, when I was 13, my best friend, Jarrel, killed himself. After he died, I drank a bunch of Bacardi and sat out on my terrace crying, confused and lost, thinking about my friends' deaths, not being with my parents or brothers, and feeling isolated instead of loved.

I felt completely alone. I doubted anyone could understand me or all that I had gone through.

After Jarrel died, I wrote many poems about guilt, death, and anger. I found that writing helped me vent emotions. But the next year, when I got to high school, my boys put me on to something even better: smoking weed. I loved it from the first.

I smoked mostly by myself. I didn't want my boys to know me too well.

We cut class, went to my boy's crib and smoked about four blunts. I took a mean pull, and after the second pull I didn't want to pass it around.

In my first two years of high school, I cut class more than 300 times and had a 55 average. I liked smoking so much because I never thought about my past or my life when I was high. I just thought about food and what I was going to do when I get home.

I smoked mostly by myself, because when I was smoking with my friends, I would come out with thoughts that I later regretted sharing. I didn't want my boys to know me too well. By 15, I was lighting up by myself in a park far from my neighborhood.

By 17, I was also drinking a lot, taking Bacardi or Hennessy to school in water bottles or drinking after school in a park. I felt lonely, frustrated, angry, and helpless.

I thought it best to drink alone so I didn't show anyone my sadness or get in trouble. When I drank I wanted to fight. If I had liquor in me, I didn't care who the dude was, I threw the hands.

In every fight, the anger of my childhood ran through my body. I didn't like who I was, but fighting, drinking, smoking, and writing were the only ways I knew of to deal with my emotions.

Then, when I was 18, I met a girl in my high school. She was a Dominican mami, a natural beauty, intelligent, loved to laugh, and had a beautiful smile. We had two classes together and eventually started dating.

Together we went shopping, to movies and amusement parks, and on picnics. At night we would sit in a park and talk for hours, or bug out in hotels, ordering Pizza Hut and watching movies and having bugged out pillow fights. We couldn't get enough of one another.

But my habits started to affect our relationship. Every time I drank, the anger I'd bottled up inside came out. On the phone, she would hear me breathing hard and ask, "Antwaun, are you OK?" I'd tell her about a fight I had, usually because I was smoking or drinking.

She realized that smoking and drinking brought out the demon in me, which we were both scared of. My girl would cry because she felt helpless to calm or console me, and I'd get mad at myself for putting her through pain.

Finally one day she told me, "Antwaun, you know I love you, right?"

"Yes!" I replied.

"I love you so much that it hurts. So you have to choose—your habits or me."

I didn't know what to say but I was thinking, "Antwaun, you're losing someone important, and for what? Choose her before you lose her!" So I told her I would stop.

I never completely stopped drinking. (My girl sometimes drank, too, and we'd have a few drinks together.) But I made a major effort to keep my cups under control. Smoking I stopped completely, because I didn't need to escape my reality when I was with her.

As I let her get to know me, she helped me let out some of the feelings I kept inside. To help her understand why I was so angry, I told her about my past.

We talked for hours about each other's pasts, even though her past wasn't like mine. She listened to me, so I felt at ease coming out with everything. I learned how to talk about my feelings rather than hide from them.

Whenever I started to cry, she would tell me, "You don't have to tell me if you're not ready," because she knew I hated crying. I would hold my head back and cover my eyes, and she would hug me and say, "It's OK to cry. I'm here. Everything is fine."

Whatever I didn't tell her about myself, she read in my articles (I was writing for a teen magazine). She kept a book of all my articles and saved them next to her journal and baby pictures. I also kept writing down all my emotions to prevent that feeling of pressure that comes from holding too

I learned how to talk about my feelings rather than hide from them.

much in. With my girl's help, I became more focused in school and my life started to look clearer. I was good.

After two years, my girl became depressed due to family issues. Then she moved away. We broke up, and I fell into a deep depression that lasted for months. I felt alone and lost. I had no clue of what I wanted to do in life.

I started drinking and smoking again and fell off in school. I didn't wash because I wanted to look like I felt: dirty and pathetic. I was always mad. I stopped writing and let my pain eat at me.

My cravings for fast food became real serious, too. Whenever I went to Micky D's I ordered up to $8 worth of food from the dollar menu. If I ordered Chinese food, I got an egg roll to go with every dish. I gained almost 20 pounds that February. Now I was depressed, confused, alone, failing school—and fat!

Gradually, I got disgusted by myself and tired of always being depressed. I was walking around in small T-shirts with a gut that hung low. My clothes felt tight. I felt like Homer Simpson with waves and a $5 T-shirt.

I started wondering, "How am I going to get over my depression? What direction am I heading in life?" I wasn't the man I wanted to be. Getting high all the time was not helping me to be at peace. Finally, I couldn't stand myself anymore. I knew I had to change.

It helped when my ex and my mom called and reminded me of my good points. "You always had a presence when you entered a room," my ex told me. My mom said she thought of me as a determined guy who never let anyone stand in his way. I began to remember my good characteristics. I am a funny, determined, caring, real dude with a passion to write and a gift for making people smile.

I decided to test myself to see if I could stop smoking weed. I started slowly, going a day without smoking by keeping myself busy. I avoided the weed spots, went to school, the library, and home.

I would get the urge to smoke at night. My anger had always given me energy. Without it, I felt lifeless and exhausted sometimes, as if the life force had drained out of me. I almost felt like if I didn't smoke or drink, I wouldn't wake up and feel alive.

But when I got the urge to drink, cry, or smoke, I took 45-minute-long showers. It's a good thing my aunt didn't have to pay the water bill! I also started taking care of myself, putting on my jewelry, which I'd left on the dresser when I was depressed, and slowing down my eating to three meals a day.

I started a workout regimen—running up and down steps, doing push-ups and sit-ups. I started to feel good physically. Seeing that I could take control of my life made my confidence grow. As I felt better, I started to keep busier and be more social. Each change made other changes happen. A year later, I'm still in the process of getting myself back.

Now I keep myself on the move—running in the morning,

going to work in the afternoon. On weekends I chill with friends who don't smoke or drink, play basketball with my sister, and take my little cousins to the movies. I don't have time to be alone and drink and smoke and reminisce about painful things.

The last time I smoked weed was four months ago. I was at my brother's apartment in Harlem. We ordered Chinese food, and one of my boys brought over an NBA game. We passed around some weed and drank orange juice and vodka while playing video games, and conversing about sports and music.

When I turned down weed, I felt powerful.

I didn't turn down the weed, because it didn't seem like a big deal to smoke one time with friends.

But the next morning I felt physically sick. I was coughing hard and spitting non-stop. That turned me off to smoking. Since then I haven't smoked weed at all.

When I saw my brother again in November and he was smoking weed, I passed it up. When I turned it down, I felt powerful. I knew I could overcome my addiction to smoking weed. I was strict with myself and I stopped.

Since then, I've also cut down smoking cigarettes (to one or two a month) and I don't drink recklessly to deal with stress — just when I'm at a party or celebration.

Both my parents have bad lungs and livers and are perfect examples of what I don't want for myself. My father is sick and paralyzed on the left side of his face but he still smokes and drinks. Now I realize that my parents may have gotten addicted to smoking, using crack, and drinking the same way I started: to cope with feelings of loneliness, anger, and fear.

I can't say I won't have any more depressions, or that the urge to drink or smoke won't ever overtake me, because I don't know what life has in store, but I know I've made a big change. I feel more in control of myself than ever before.

Antwaun was 21 when he wrote this story.

Kenly Dillard

Last Man Standing

By Russell Morse

Walden House Adolescent Drug Treatment and Mental Health Facility in California is a one-year program. I was there for two.

The intake manager (nicknamed Dusty because of his preference for Rustler's cigars and his indifference to hygiene), picked me up from San Francisco's juvenile hall on a hot July day in his electric blue Ford Tempo. My knight in shining armor, he rescued me from the cold, lonely world of juvenile hall and delivered me to a place where I knew not what to expect.

I was fortunate in just being considered for a placement. I had committed an array of crimes that qualified me as a menace to society, and probation could have sent me someplace serious. Thankfully, probation officers and judges saw that at the root of my criminality and destructive patterns was a serious substance abuse problem. Someone felt like I deserved a shot at redemption and it came in the form of Walden House.

In my extended stay at Walden House, I was continually disciplined. The counselors hit me with the hardest kinds of consequences they could deliver. I was threatened with permanent discharge more times than I can remember. They broke me down and built me up over and over again. In those 24 months, I underwent the most intense and excruciating period of transformation that I'll probably ever experience. I both hated and loved it.

The company was great. We were a band of unruly, delinquent drug addicts with violent tendencies thrown into a "therapeutic community." We attended regular therapy sessions in which every move you made was analyzed and related to your "old behaviors." We were taught to call each other "brother" and were ordered to give each other hugs.

Thankfully, someone felt like I deserved a shot at redemption.

Walden House was not a locked facility. Anyone could leave whenever he wanted and, sadly, most did. Often the weekend coordinator spoke of our odds. He would say, "Look to your left and look to your right. If you're here in a year, those people won't be." The ones I shared most of my time with were those who managed to stick it out to the end.

Sean P. got there the day before I did. We'd spent some time in the hall together. It was nice to see a familiar face the day I rolled up. Sean was an odd fellow who made car sounds as he walked ("vrooom…vrooom... screeech!"). Toward the end of his stay, he convinced himself that he was Chinese. When he got upset, he started speaking a strange Asian-sounding language of his own creation.

Harvey L. (we used no last names) was the Filipino from Daly City, California who wanted to be a soul singer. He would memorize the words to slow jams and sing them with a tear lingering on his eyelid while he wrote poetic love letters to distant girlfriends.

Doug D. would read Kurt Vonnegut or Paul Bowles novels until 3 o'clock in the morning and then barge into my room to discuss the insanity of our existence. He held fast to the dream that he would one day grace the screen as a porn star.

Luis K. was one of my best friends. His girlfriend had his baby while he was inside and he built his future on being a good father. Luis was one who I could cry and laugh with—sometimes both at the same time.

Nate O. was the wise one of the camp. He had managed to work his way up the levels of the program in record time, and spent most of his time out of the house. I got in trouble for preparing a set of fake documents for him to take to court so he could leave early.

Geovanni W. was another of my good friends. He was dealt more than his share of hardships in his young life, but he still managed to make me laugh when I needed it. His mother was murdered when he was 2, and shortly after his father was arrested on felony charges and sent to prison. His father got out, but because he often violated his parole, he was in and out of county jail. Geo used to go visit him there. Geo's whole life outside of Walden House was built around his grandmother, whom he called "mom," and what he felt was his duty to look after her.

Those were a select few members of our clan. We spent every minute of every day together, war-storying, growing, teaching, and learning. There was a sense of camaraderie in that place that I don't think I'll ever enjoy anywhere else.

The staff often said that one day someone would be smoking crack in my kitchen and I would have to dig deep to find the strength to kick them out of my house. "For what?" I would ask myself. "What if it's raining? Do you know how hard it is to get a crack pipe lit in a storm?"

The counselors called snitching "supporting." We were told that we were really helping our brothers when we ratted on them. If we didn't snitch, we were enabling them and keeping them sick.

Either way, "smoking crack in your kitchen" became a metaphor for every little thing that I did to help my brothers out—looking the other way while my roommate smoked cigarettes out the window, or playing lookout while a friend made "underground" (a term used for illegal or against the rules) calls from the kitchen phone. I was constantly dubbed "poison in the community." They told me that I would never survive outside of the container they provided. It got to the point where I felt like smoking crack in my kitchen.

But eventually I got it. And when I did, they were more than glad to let me go. I guess you could say I had overstayed my welcome. I had no trouble obliging…well, that's not entirely true.

We were a band of unruly, delinquent drug addicts with violent tendencies thrown into a "therapeutic community."

See, I had grown fond of the place. I didn't regard it as an oppressive, captive environment. By the time I left, I thought of it as home. I'd made great friends there and changed in magical ways. I learned to deal with my pain and cry when I needed to. The staff members, as often as they tormented me, did so because they genuinely cared about me and wanted to see me succeed in this cruel world. They saw that I had gifts and wanted to see me go on to live a happy, productive life. Having people like that in my life was new to me and I was going to miss it. Plus, I was scared.

I had nearly two years clean and sober at my time of discharge. I wasn't sure I could keep that up on my own. I didn't want to go back to jail, but crime was something that I lived and died by before I came there. That was how I ate. I didn't have a home to go back to. I was alone in my journey and I accepted that. But I was scared.

On June 1, they turned me loose. They had a farewell dinner for me where everyone I loved and cared about gathered together to say their goodbyes and wish me the best of luck. I was toasted and roasted until the sun came up and then it was really over. I left the gates of Walden House a free man. I could smoke, curse, and go where I pleased, and I wasn't obligated to give anyone a hug. I could have gone and copped some dope or stolen a car. But I didn't.

Instead, I went to my aunt's house and tossed and turned because the mattress was too damn comfortable. And the next morning, I awoke a free, clean and sober, brand new man ready to face the day. I went and did everything I had only dreamt of from behind Walden House walls.

I enrolled in San Francisco State University, landed a regular job, found my own apartment and got laid. I was living the dream.

Not a day went by, however, that I didn't want to drink, get high, or commit some heinous act that would land me back in jail. I was alienated by this brave new world. It wasn't the San Francisco I remembered. I told myself, "I don't belong here." I sat in college classes and fought the fact that I was a college student. I paid bills and felt like an everyday Joe, a square. But I stuck it out because I knew I had fought hard and deserved every second of success.

My peers, on the other hand, didn't fare so well. Harvey went on a crack binge, stole his mom's car, and kidnapped his ex-girlfriend. The authorities caught up with him and he's back in a cage somewhere.

I saw Luis in front of a used clothing store on Haight Street, trying to hustle up some money for a burrito and a sack of herb. When I asked him when was the last time he had seen his daughter, he couldn't recall. I wanted to cry on his shoulder, but he wasn't that Luis anymore.

Geo called me out of the blue to tell me that his grandmother had died and he wasn't sure what he was living for anymore. I called him back a few days later, but his grandfather told me that he was in Santa Rita County Jail, on the other side of the same glass he had sat behind when he used to visit his father.

I run into Doug on Market Street every once in a while and he always tells me of his schemes to get rich through big money dope deals. I hooked him up with a local porn director, but he never followed through. He's still in Walden House, but he's 18 so he's in adult services, trying to hide the fact that he's just getting over for a place to live.

I heard recently that Sean was doing a nine-month bid for a dope case. He sent me a word-of-mouth message that he was doing all right and wanted me to "stay up, playa."

Nate was going strong for a while, but he's slipped back into the life of drugs and crime. He was fretting earlier tonight because he kicked over his glass bong and it shattered on the hardwood floor. I haven't caught him smoking crack in my kitchen yet, and I don't know what I'd do if I did.

On New Year's, I'll be celebrating 32 months since I last put poison in my body. I jaywalk on occasion, but other than that I'm a law-abiding citizen.

New Year's Day, God willing, I'll be celebrating 32 months since I last put poison in my body. I just finished my first semester at San Francisco State, and I'm registered for the next. I jaywalk on occasion, but other than that, I'm a law-abiding citizen. I lead writing workshops in the same unit at juvenile hall where I was once a detainee. I got off probation shortly after my release and the law can't touch me unless I give them reason.

So why have I fared so well? How have I watched my peers drop on all sides of me and still kept moving in the right direction? I'm not sure. I just wake up every morning and ask God to give me the strength to make it through another day clean and sober, to make the right decisions, and to treat others with the love and respect that they deserve.

I owe a lot to Walden House. And even though my friends have fallen, I owe a lot to them. It's sad to see what's happened to them, but I still keep a candle burning in the hopes that they'll get to where they need to be—out of the cage and living the dream.

I could still use a hug every once in a while, though.

Russell went on to become an editor at New American Media.

This story was originally published in YO!, a magazine by and for youth in San Francisco, California. Copyright © YO! Reprinted with permission.

Terrence Taylor

Hooked on Heroin

By Anonymous

Talia poured out the contents of the bag onto a hand-held mirror, divided the caramel-colored powder into two neat lines, and used a straw to snort one. Then she handed me the mirror.

I didn't know what the powder was, but I figured it couldn't hurt to try it. I'd snorted coke before and been fine. I ignored the fact that she wasn't telling me what it was and snorted. It burned the inside of my nose enough to make me tear, and it was bitter in my throat.

I couldn't feel anything at first. Then all the muscles in my body relaxed. It was an effort to lift my arm or cross my legs. I felt a warm flush in my face and everything seemed kind of hazy. When I moved my head quickly, my vision blurred.

I was happy for what seemed like the first time in years. If the apocalypse happened at that very moment, I'd have enjoyed the music on Talia's stereo anyway. I'd never felt anything like this from a drug or on my own. I lay down on her shag rug, and embraced being high on heroin for the first time. I was 15.

I'd been depressed ever since a fire damaged my family's Brooklyn apartment when I was in 8th grade. My parents, my brother, and I were homeless for four months, living at my uncle's house, a hotel, and a homeless shelter in Harlem.

My blissful innocence was reduced to ash in the fire, along with everything we owned. Feeling hopeless and depressed, I figured that there was no reason to go to school, since everything I worked for could be gone in a second. I started looking for any outlet that would make me forget what had happened.

Toward the end of 8th grade, I found it at a friend's party. We were standing in a circle on Sandy's deck and everyone was excited because someone had brought weed. I watched some kid take a drag on the joint, inhale deeply, and hold his breath.

I'd never tried drugs before, and I kept thinking that I'd become instantly addicted or brain dead, like the cheesy anti-drug commercials claimed. When I was handed the joint, I swallowed all fear, took a drag and inhaled.

I felt oddly proud of myself for disregarding my parents, teachers, and every other authority that had tried to discourage me from using drugs. I started smoking weed every week. I also started smoking cigarettes and drinking every weekend with friends.

When I started freshman year at Fashion Industries HS, I met a bunch of people who used drugs, and we ended up cutting classes and putting our lunch money together to buy drugs and alcohol.

I loved that being high or drunk made me forget the fire and everything else that worried me. When I was trashed, I didn't feel shy or alone. I didn't feel like the whole world was against me. I didn't feel a thing.

After Talia introduced me to heroin, we'd meet up at the

school bathroom a few times a month to use. Soon I needed more and more heroin to feel as good as I did in the beginning. Instead of just using heroin whenever Talia had it, I started looking for it and using it more often. Every other week turned into every other day, which turned into every day.

After about six months of using, I needed to snort three bags of heroin a day to feel normal. When I didn't have any, I would get so depressed and sick that I thought I was dying.

All I cared about was heroin—where I could get it, how much, and when I could do it. I had stopped going to class, and I only spoke to my parents to say good morning and ask for money for lunch (which went to drugs).

When I was trashed, I didn't feel shy or alone. I didn't feel like the whole world was against me. I didn't feel a thing.

After I'd been using for seven months, I started dating my boyfriend. I told him I'd done drugs but I didn't tell him I'd get loaded before we'd meet up to go to the movies or walk through the park. I was afraid if he knew, he'd try to make me stop.

After 11 months, my mom got worried about me isolating myself and acting differently. She sent me to a therapist, Debbie, who said that everything I told her would be confidential. I felt the need to tell someone about my addiction, so I ended up telling Debbie.

"How often do you use?" she asked.

"Well, I started out doing a little, now I do more."

"How much more are we talking about?"

"Well, like three little baggies a day."

"Maya, I'm sorry, but when you're potentially hurting yourself, I have to tell your parents," she said.

All I could think was they were going to try to get me to stop, and I didn't want to stop. Debbie gave me a five-day deadline, so I reluctantly agreed to have a meeting with her and my mother on my 16th birthday.

I made sure to get really high before my mom and I left the house, since I'd probably be watched 24/7 afterwards. I felt great. Even if I had been heading to the electric chair, it would have been a pleasant experience.

"Mrs. Martinez, you do know why I called this meeting?" Debbie asked.

"I was hoping you'd tell me," my mom said.

"Maya, maybe you can fill your mother in?"

I wanted to punch Debbie in the face. I was never good at being subtle so I just blurted it out. "Mom, I've been doing heroin for a year," I said.

My mom sat there in her swivel office chair and started to cry. I usually felt horrible when I made her cry, but with the drugs I only felt bliss.

"I looked up inpatient rehab services for you, Mrs. Martinez, where Maya can go," Debbie said.

That was the end of my freedom. When we got home, my parents had me on complete lockdown until I left a few days later for Arms Acres Rehab Facility in upstate New York.

By the morning I had to leave, I was out of the last bit of heroin I'd kept hidden under my bed. When I started to feel sick, I desperately searched the house and found my mother's Codeine painkillers. I swallowed four pills, then crushed and snorted two. I felt better, but it wasn't as good as heroin.

The pills got me through the trip upstate, the tears and kisses goodbye and the first day and night. I felt the withdrawal for the first time the next morning. My entire body hurt, every bone ached, I was nauseous, and I went from freezing cold to burning hot. My nose started running, and all I wanted was something to make the pain stop.

My first days in rehab were horrible. I'd refuse to wake up on time or talk when they went around the circle asking for everyone's name, age, and drug of choice. At night, I'd try to rock myself to sleep, crying from the pain of withdrawal and homesickness.

After four days, I saw that I wasn't going to get out of there unless I cooperated. I realized that using didn't rid my mind of depression, anger, and emotional pain—it had only suppressed those feelings.

After I was clean for about a week, all my emotions came out of me randomly, for the wrong reasons and at the wrong time. I'd get angry when my mother called to say she loved me, I'd feel sorry when my boyfriend called to say he loved me, and I'd laugh when someone was pouring out her soul about hitting "rock bottom."

I started to realize how broken I was. I had no confidence in myself, and I had no idea who I was anymore. I finally realized that I was a heroin addict.

After two weeks, the staff gave me an evaluation and decided I was ready to be discharged. I had to go to an outpatient program three or four times a week. And my parents and I decided I should go to a different high school, since there was no way I could stay clean at Fashion Industries, my old school. I hadn't been to school for months, and I was scared to go back.

When I started at South Brooklyn Community HS, I had no friends. But I started bringing home grades above a C and started to gain a tiny bit more confidence in myself and my abilities. Gradually, I started to make new friends and speak up in class.

In February, my art teacher took our class to a museum in Manhattan. When the trip was over, he dismissed us a block away from Fashion Industries, right before school let out.

After being clean for 11 months, I thought I was strong enough to visit my friends, as long as I didn't see Talia. But then I heard her yelling out my name.

I was happy to see her, but I wanted to run away from her at the same time. She looked a little skinnier than I remembered, and her cheeks were sunken in. I told her that my 17th birthday was the next day, and she said she had a special surprise for me.

I could have told her no, because I was trying to stay clean. Instead, I followed her into the train to Brooklyn, telling her "I can't, I can't."

I followed her to a car where she handed some shady-looking guy money and took a small bundle from him. We went to a nearby McDonald's bathroom, where she set up the lines on a small mirror and rolled up a dollar bill.

"Maya, it's your birthday tomorrow, and you should live a little," she said. "You can go back to your boring little clean life tomorrow."

As horrible as it sounds, I agreed with her. Life was pretty boring just going to school, doing homework, and being in bed by 11 p.m. I pushed the arguments about why I shouldn't do it out of my head and took the mirror and the dollar bill.

The heroin made me feel a million times better than I had in months. I'd missed being high, and I was in love with feeling lighter and free of stress and worry. I never wanted it to end.

> *"It's your birthday tomorrow, and you should live a little," she said. "You can go back to your boring little clean life tomorrow."*

We hung out for a while, both high as kites, talking about whatever random thoughts popped into our heads.

The next morning, I cried for half an hour in bed under my blanket. I remembered that my boyfriend was going to take me out for my birthday that day. He'd been there for me throughout my whole ordeal, and I felt like I had betrayed his trust, along with everyone else's.

When we met, he kept asking me what was wrong. He noticed that I couldn't look him in the eye. Finally, I blurted out that I had relapsed. He sat quietly and kept his head down, and I started crying again. I told him I wasn't going to do it again.

But two months later, I convinced him to do heroin with me. I thought I needed to do it just one more time, and I wanted us to do it together. I felt like that would make it OK. I wouldn't have to hide anything from him.

We got high in a library bathroom. Afterwards we took a walk and talked for hours. We joked, we kept telling each other how much we loved each other, and we made out in front of a bunch of people.

We both thought it was a great experience, but the next day we talked and agreed not to do it again. We knew we couldn't live that way if we were going to have some kind of future.

Still, a few weeks later I tried to convince him to get high with me again. But this time he refused. He didn't want me to do it alone, either, so I didn't. I didn't want to make him angry.

After a couple of months the urge to get high faded, and I became more myself again. I started to see how much of my life I'd been wasting by using. Heroin clouded reality, and it kept me from experiencing things like most people do. I realized that the way I'd acted while on drugs still bothered

I realized I couldn't do heroin without ruining everything else in my life.

me. I decided to write about my addiction for an English paper, figuring that I'd purge it from my mind.

When my teacher read it, she told me I was a great writer and that I should try to write a book about my life. I'd always kept journals, but for the first time I could see myself becoming a writer.

I realized I couldn't do heroin without ruining everything else in my life. I knew that I had no control over it. I'll always love the way it made me feel, but the price is too much for a temporary high. I could lose my boyfriend and the trust I've gained with everyone in my life, and screw up my progress at school and with myself.

It's been three years now since I left rehab, and about two years since I relapsed. I don't do any kind of drug anymore, although I still drink occasionally. I'm due to graduate this coming June, and I've never been more confident and outspoken than I am today.

Heroin tore me to pieces, but sometimes I'll still think about using when I'm stressed or mad. I'm pretty sure if I came in contact with Talia or the other people from my past, they could convince me to do it again. I figure it's best to avoid the temptation by staying away from them.

I don't regret what I went through, but I can't allow myself to screw up my life again. I've gotten too far to mess it up just to get high one more time.

The author was in high school when she wrote this story.

Shamel Allison

My Battle to Quit

By Ashunte Hunt

I was 14 and living in my second group home when I first smoked a blunt. I was outside on campus and it was a nice cool day. The sun was out and a breeze was blowing. It seemed like a good time to kick back and smoke a blunt with a friend. All my life I was always around people who smoked, so I didn't think it was a problem.

When I took my first hit I felt a calming, mellow sensation that I'd never felt in my life. I wanted to feel that way all the time.

After that, whenever I'd chill with my friends we'd smoke weed, play video games, and play basketball. Smoking helped me be accepted, and it also helped me deal with all the stress I was going through living away from my family.

After a while, all the weed I was smoking didn't make me feel as good as it had at first, so I started smoking more. I'd get mad when I wanted to smoke but couldn't.

Teachers and staff from my group home would come to me and tell me that I needed to stop, but I didn't listen to them. I felt that they didn't understand the stress and pain that I was going through, dealing with the death of my parents, being separated from my biological family, and missing my long-lost sister.

I didn't know how to do the things I wanted to do, like become a peaceful child or find my family. So I did whatever I thought would help me. In the past I'd tried things like listening to music and writing poetry to keep my composure and get my head off of whatever got me upset. But smoking was even better.

Weed calmed me down and kept me from doing something that could have sent me to jail. It soothed my anger, and brought me to a level where I could slow down and think about what I was doing before I did it.

Marijuana (aka Mary) became my good friend. Mary was the only person I felt understood me. She took the time to listen to me when nobody else wanted to listen, and the only advice she gave was, "Stay in connection with me." And I did, I did for a long time. She was a reflection of the peaceful, more understanding side of me.

Weed soothed my anger, and brought me to a level where I could slow down and think about what I was doing before I did it.

But after a while, Mary became a real problem in my life. I'd gone from smoking one or two blunts a day to three or four a day. At times I would smoke more. It was getting me in trouble, because I was starting to slack on a lot of things like schoolwork or my curfew.

I started to lose interest in some of the things that I used to do like swimming, playing pool, and trying to better my basketball skills. I was burning a big hole in my pocket from buying the weed, and people started to look at me funny, saying that they knew I could do better.

I knew I could, too, but I was caught in the middle trying to figure out what I wanted to do. The staff kept telling me that I should stop, but that was harder than it sounded.

There were drug counselors working in my group home, so I went and spoke to one and requested to be put in an inpatient rehab. I thought that my drug counselor could send me somewhere so I could get help with my addiction.

I wanted to quit and I knew I needed to get away from everything that I'd been around that had started my addiction in the first place. I wanted to get some help before I hit rock bottom, before nobody cared anymore and they'd just let me waste my life away smoking weed.

It took almost a year before the drug counselor told me that they'd found a rehab that would accept me. It was in upstate New York and I'd be there for two months.

When I got there, I was skeptical, and I didn't feel welcomed. In less than a week I already wanted to leave. They had me doing six groups a day, talking about stuff like what problems you started having at the time you were doing drugs and how you felt about everything.

I didn't feel comfortable sharing personal information with people I didn't know from a hole in the wall. I didn't want to go into detail about my life and the things that caused me to smoke, like losing my family.

I had come to rehab because I was looking for strategic, practical steps to quit before it was too late. But the staff wanted to change your whole character, like they could do that in two months.

After a few weeks I'd gotten familiar with the program and at times I would share in some groups, when I felt comfortable. But I still didn't do everything they wanted. I didn't want to be looked at differently because of my experiences.

The other people who shared had stories that were similar to mine, but I didn't want their sympathy or those fake, "I understand the pain you're going through," statements. I didn't think anyone could understand, and I wanted to avoid all of that before my anger took control.

The staff also gave us packets to fill out that I really didn't like. The questions they asked were very personal. They wanted you to record all the major things that are hard for you to share and tell them like it was no problem. I rushed through all of them just to get it over with.

They asked questions like, "Have you ever been molested or raped?" and "How often do you masturbate?" There was another question that got me real pissed off: "Have you ever had sex with one of your family members?" I wanted to go to my counselor and shove that packet up her anus, but I regained my composure and brushed it off.

Staff at the rehab center told me it's bad to be around the same people and places, but I had no choice but to go back to the group home.

Still, just being in a quiet, less populated place helped me get in touch with myself and deal with my smoking problem. I started thinking about everything I've been through, good or bad, and I drew my own blueprint for how I was going to rebuild my foundation.

The blueprint consisted of steps that I could take to keep myself in check. They were things like: quit cigarettes, still hang out with my friends but leave whenever they start smoking weed, and, most importantly, keep myself busy. It was an outline to keep me sober, and I had no doubts that it would work.

Before I knew it I was down to my last week. I was excited to finally leave. I couldn't wait to tell people about my experience with the wilderness. And the first thing I wanted to do was play basketball.

But then another feeling came to me, like my mind was trying to warn me about something. I paused in the middle of writing a poem and had a premonition. It played in my mind like this: I would get back to the group home (the place where I started smoking), go through a battle with myself, and then lose and start smoking again.

That scared me, because I knew if I picked up the habit again I'd have a harder time recovering. I didn't want to have to go through anything like this ever again.

Staff at the rehab center told me it's bad to be around the same people, places, and things, but they didn't acknowledge that I had no choice but to go back to the group home. Facing my return was harder than going up to rehab.

I started to get more anxious as every day passed by, but the blueprint I'd made gave me courage. I took it one day at a time until the day I was heading back to my group home.

At the group home, I started to do what I do best and that was to chill. But it was hard having to go back to the same place, see most of the same people, and deal with the same things that I dealt with before rehab. I had to deal with people always bringing up things that I used to do, like the fights I used to have and how I used to flip out to the point that I had to get restrained by staff.

When I'd go outside to enjoy the weather, I always saw somebody smoking weed or drinking on the campus and that also made the process a whole lot harder. I'd leave one place where people were using drugs only to run into another crowd of people who were smoking, too. And it wasn't like I could walk off campus and go somewhere that was drug free.

Still, my blueprint was in full effect and I stood strong to it for three or four months. Then I relapsed.

I went to my best friend's house and her brother asked me if I knew how to roll. I told him yeah and he asked me to roll his blunt. I thought, "What the heck, why not?" and rolled it for him.

Boy, was that the wrong move, because I ended up smoking with him. When he passed me the blunt I just took it without thinking and started smoking. When I realized what I was doing it was already too late. I had the weed in my system. Ever since then, it's been a back-and-forth thing with me smoking.

I've been stressed about a lot of things. My ex-girlfriend is pregnant and she says the baby's mine. To tell you the truth I didn't want to keep it because I'm not ready to take care of a child, especially when I don't have a job or a high school diploma. But she has all the control so I can't get mad if she decides to have my child.

Even worse, I've been having flashbacks again about the death of my parents, which is part of what led me to smoke in the first place.

Sometimes the staff try to give me lectures about their own tough experiences, but I don't want to hear what they went through. It would just get me stuck on how messed up my life is, and how I wish that it was never like that. I don't want to dwell on my problems. I want to try to find ways to change and make things better.

When I went to rehab, I was looking for help to stop smoking weed so I could do better in life. When I'm in a peaceful area, away from the group home, I feel very comfortable and no thoughts of smoking weed come to my head. Just like in rehab, I have my moments of clarity and keep a peaceful mindset.

But in the group home, those stresses I'm facing make it hard. I do try to talk about my problems, but so far that hasn't helped. I hope I'll be able to stop smoking before I do something I regret. But I think that until something changes, it's going to be a struggle.

Ashunte was 17 when he wrote this story.
He went on to college.

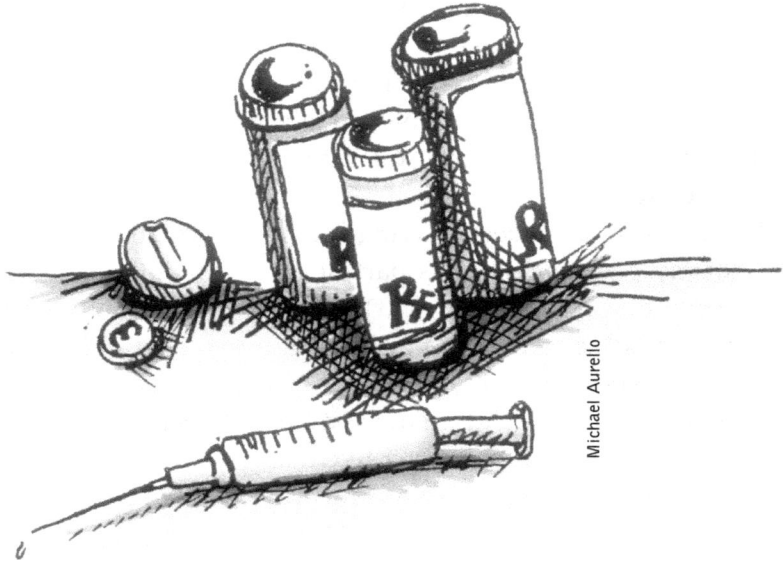

Michael Aurello

What Drugs Do To You (Even the Legal Ones)

To understand more about how drugs affect teenagers, we interviewed Dr. James A. Hall, co-director of the adolescent medicine program at the University of Iowa in Iowa City. Hall is a professor of pediatrics, social work, public health, and nursing, and has spent many years researching teenage drug use.

Q: How do I know if I have a problem with drugs or alcohol?

A: There are several warning signs that drug dependence is destroying your ability to live a healthy, happy life:

If you drink or use drugs when you're alone, can't trust yourself to get through certain situations without having to use, or can't remember things that happened when you were high, you should seek help.

If your drug use and hangovers cause problems for you at work or in school (being late, getting loaded instead of studying, falling behind, or getting kicked out), you are also on dangerous ground.

Another sign you are in trouble is when drugs begin destroying your relationships: Your friends or parents are on your back about your temper, mood swings, unreliability, or inability to pay attention and stay alert. Or you lie to people about what you've been doing and prefer getting high to being with people who care about you.

You need help if you have to get high in order to feel good or have fun, or if you turn to pills, pot, or alcohol after fights or confrontations to calm down or feel better.

Building up a tolerance is a sign of physical addiction: When you need more and more of something in order to get the same effect, you are getting addicted.

Q: What's so bad about smoking weed or popping pills like cold medicines?

A: Adolescence is a time where you figure out who you are as an individual in society. You go from having external controls (other people telling you what to do) to internal controls (making decisions and thinking things through for yourself). Kids who are on drugs—even marijuana—can't handle these challenges very well because

> *You need help if you have to get high in order to feel good or have fun, or if you turn to pills, pot, or alcohol to calm down.*

they aren't able to figure out their problems and interpret the world with a clear head.

If you spend a lot of time smoking, you will have delays in learning how to cope with life and how to solve problems, and be slower in developing the confidence and skills you need to overcome the obstacles every adult encounters. When you come down, all the same problems are still there.

Also, many studies show marijuana use interferes with learning. You're slower to understand and respond to things when you're high and get really bad at remembering things. This makes it more difficult to do well in school, to keep yourself safe, and to analyze situations so you can make good decisions.

Even over-the-counter medications can be harmful if you're taking more than you're supposed to take, or taking them for a reason other than the problem that the medicines are designed to help (like taking cold medicine when you don't have a cold). Many over-the-counter drugs can be every bit as dangerous as street drugs if you take too much.

Q: Is there anyone I can talk to about my drug use who won't broadcast my business?

A: The best person to start with is your medical doctor. Make an appointment and bring a list of questions to ask him or her. Doctors are obligated to keep what you tell them completely private and confidential. Drug use alone is not something they have to report to anyone. There are exceptions to this confidentiality guarantee, though: If you tell the doctor you want to hurt yourself or harm someone else, or if you say you are taking drugs to kill yourself, the doctor will report this to the authorities and tell your parent or guardian.

Also, if the doctor sees that you are being abused or neglected, or you tell him that you are, he has to make a report. But in most cases, doctors have to keep anything you say, and everything about your treatment, confidential. In many states, kids can even seek and receive drug rehab without permission from parents or guardians. Ask your doctor or a local drug treatment provider what the rules are in your state.

Q: What's the difference between taking street drugs and the medications doctors prescribe?

A: Lots of teenagers do street drugs or use over-the-counter drugs because they have an underlying condition such as depression, attention deficit hyperactivity disorder, or a learning disorder. They medicate themselves to get more energy, to focus or concentrate, or to feel calmer or happier. The problem is that illegal drugs have many unpredictable side effects that can make you extremely sick. Also, you are likely to build up a tolerance—if you stop using them, you crash. Reality can become unbearable and withdrawal can be agony.

Drugs that your doctor prescribes are better because their effects are more predictable. Scientists have tested them for purity and quality, established safe dosage amounts, and studied their side effects. Also, the doctor monitors your consumption to make sure the drugs are working right and that you don't take too much.

It's an especially bad idea to take illegal or over-the-counter drugs if you are already on antidepressants or other psychiatric medications. Combining these substances can make you very sick in many different ways. For example, if you are already taking Ritalin and smoke a lot of marijuana, you might become depressed. Using a lot of amphetamines (meth, or "uppers"), combined with drinking, smoking marijuana, and going without sleep, can provoke psychotic episodes.

Michael Aurello

Ecstasy Proved to be Anything But

By M. Lopez

I was sitting in the car with the sexiest man in existence, but I kept glancing at the clock...27 minutes...35...40, nothing yet. We started kissing, but after 10 passionate minutes of window-fogging intimacy, still nothing. I was thinking, "It's been almost an hour! What a complete waste of $25."

Then—WHOA, what was that? Shook it off. Then—WOW, there it goes again. OK, I was definitely not imagining it. I sighed in euphoric delight.

My thug didn't notice my permanent grin, or how I was draped on the headrest. Or how my eyes were slits of glassy black diamonds, completely dilated. As my man drove me back to the West Village, a neighborhood in New York City, I felt dazed. I started thinking of world peace. I gave some serious thought to donating large sums of money to needy overseas charities. We pulled up to the corner. Smooched. I didn't wanna move.

Then I did. It felt so good to move and touch. Finally, I popped open the door, swooped out, and gleefully looked around. A familiar shape caught my eye. I focused. Good, it was one of my girlfriends. I slowly glided over in her direction and embraced her. She laughed, "Girl, what's up?" With a slight grind of my teeth and a deep breath I replied, "Girl, I'm rollin'."

I spent the rest of that night in my very first ecstasy dream, hovering around the West Village in search of stimulation, some OJ, and a bust-down on a Newport. I couldn't believe how absolutely wonderful the feeling was. I felt flooded with compassion and empathy for those around me, and 110% more sensitive in every particle of my body. Rollin' was fab—nothin' like it anywhere.

E was the only time I felt euphoric, and I didn't want to give that up.

This was my first trip in a long chain of pill-popping passion. For months on end, I found time to roll nearly every weekend. My friends and I went to clubs and anywhere else we could find loud music and sexy men. Plus, I kept up a regular regimen of green Dutches with my preferred herbal filling.

I believed this newfound friend of mine was sent from above. (Where else could these little love drops of joy be developed?) I popped again and again, double- or even triple-stacking pills.

Even though E is not physically addictive, I couldn't stand to end the high. On E, I didn't focus on the negative in my life, like I usually do. Instead, I felt like I had total control.

But at the end of each night, I would remember that I've had a pretty hard life, with lots of physical and emotional pain that I still haven't dealt with. So each time I popped, I found myself thinking about how to get my next roll.

While all tingly on cloud nine, I'd make some real practical decisions on how to better my circumstances. Of course, the next day I realized that all my wonderful ideas were actually unrealistic and full of tiny, gloomy holes that I couldn't stop dwelling on.

I'm usually an emotional person, so a couple of post-pill crying spells here and there seemed like nothing. But after a while, I started noticing I had really unpleasant mornings after my li'l pill.

I felt irritable and severely sensitive. I'd find myself writing in my tear-streaked journal, jotting down how cruel people can be and how overwhelmingly alone I felt. (That's called depression.)

I had no idea what was ailing my moods…or so I told myself. Actually, I knew for sure that the ecstasy was adding drama to my already complicated life. The E was also affecting me physically. I was losing weight because I barely had an appetite while on E, and I had no energy whatsoever the next day. This wasn't good.

So I did what any resourceful young person would do in that kind of situation—I phoned a friend. This friend happened to know a lot about youth and drug use, from formal education and experience. And she has yet to steer me in the wrong direction. So I decided to trust her with the truth of what I was doing and how I was feeling.

My friend told me why E was affecting my life and health so negatively. She said E works by interacting with the part of your brain that controls emotion, causing it to produce and release much more "happy juice" than normal. After making you giddy and euphoric for hours on end, your body's "happy juice" quickly drops from very high to very low. This is called crashing.

Crashing can result in severe depression or exhaustion (partly because the user has probably been very active while high, sweating a lot and not eating or drinking). The more E you take, the stronger the negative effects.

Most people develop a higher tolerance for the drug and have to take more and more, making crashes much worse. Plus, she told me that there are all types of complications from E, from brain problems to heart attacks and seizures to having long-term depression even after you stop using.

Of course, after learning all this, I felt a little bit apprehensive about continuing my heavy usage. I didn't want the nights without sleep and days without appetite, or the hour-long crying spells and depression that followed a night of rolling. I knew I couldn't keep going as I was. But I didn't want to stop, either. E was the only time I felt euphoric, and I didn't want to give that up.

After thinking it over, I decided it would be best for my health and my pockets to roll a little less. "Maybe once or twice a month…a half a pill here or there won't hurt," I told myself.

I tried to change my life so I was happy as much as possible without a pill.

It really wasn't as hard as I thought to stop the constant popping. I convinced myself to hold off by telling myself, "Wait 'til you're all hype about it again, and just smoke, smoke, smoke those green Dutches until then."

I also tried to change my life so I was happy as much as possible without a pill. I started to get lots of sleep and good eats, surrounded myself with loads of chipper, upbeat friends, and spent every sober second dealing with what's really important in life (like how to get more cuties to get out of their throwbacks and fitteds).

Obviously I'm not yet the picture of health, and it's probably not the greatest thing in the world for me to keep rollin', but at least I've cut back. I'm not getting as depressed anymore.

When I do use E, I try to remind myself that it's just a drug, and that the world won't really be different when I come back down.

The writer was 19 when she wrote this story.

Terrence Taylor

Becoming Someone Else

By Daniel Verzhbo

I remember looking out the plane's window and seeing how beautiful America looked. I couldn't wait to be in New York City among all those tall buildings. I expected America to be a very good country. I pictured my mom and me having a good life, ready to overcome anything.

But when we got to America, it wasn't as perfect as it looked. In Russia I was a good, quiet kid, always staying at home and spending time with my family. But in America, I started to become a different Daniel.

When we got to New York my mom got a job as a cleaning lady, but a few months later she got hurt and couldn't work anymore. Since we had no money to pay the rent, we had to go into a shelter for homeless people. When we moved into the shelter I was very sad and depressed. I started to miss my family back in Russia. I felt sorry for myself, and even more for my mother.

Our neighborhood in Brooklyn smelled like straight garbage and old buildings. Every other night I heard these loud noises that always woke me up. I thought it was fireworks at first. I also heard a lot of ambulances. "There must be lots of accidents around here," I thought. Later I realized that the fireworks were gunshots and the accidents were bullet wounds.

At first, I tried to stay away from meeting new people. I felt unsure of myself in this new life, and I didn't have the confidence to go out and look for friends. I was shy and used to keeping to myself. In Russia, I never needed to meet new people because I had my family. There were six of us and we were like a team, always together and always looking out for each other. I felt safe, and knew that with my family behind me I could accomplish anything I set my mind to.

But now I was in America, and I didn't have all that to back me up. I didn't even know the language very well. Now that I only had my mother I was lonely and bored.

I got tired of sitting in the small room that my mother and I had to share. I also got tired of trying to tell myself that I had something, because I really had nothing. No family, no friends— no life.

One day as I was shooting baskets by myself a couple of kids came over. "Yo, you look like you play ball, you want to run a full court with us?" one of them asked.

I was scared, and I barely understood him because my English was so poor. But I knew the words "full court." In my school kids would always say those words when they were play- ing ball.

I thought this could be a new way to meet friends. But I played horribly and barely even scored. I was angry at myself. "I let the opportunity slide right by me," I thought. "I played so badly nobody will even talk to me."

But after the game one kid introduced himself, and I met all of them one by one. I was relieved to see that they weren't going to rob me. I started playing basketball and hanging out with those guys on a regular basis, and I started to feel more comfortable around them.

Finally, I had friends. They opened the door for me to the real world, outside of my room. I started to feel good about myself. I felt like I was finally fitting in in America.

I started to do the things my friends did, like smoke cigarettes, and steal small things like candy from the store. I thought, "It's just candy. What's the worst that could happen?"

After a few months my mother and I moved to a nicer shelter in Sheepshead Bay, another neighborhood in Brooklyn, and I made a new friend. Darren lived in my building, and hanging out with him made me feel comfortable about myself. I could relate to him because we'd both been through a lot of the same things. We both had single mothers and didn't have a lot of money.

Darren introduced me to his crew. They were mad cool, and at first it felt good to be around them. Hanging out with them was like being part of a huge family. I felt protected. But the crew also got me involved in some bad stuff like smoking weed, fighting, and stealing.

The first time I smoked weed I thought that it would make me cough, like cigarettes, but it felt smooth as I inhaled it. I felt that "chillin feelin" (as my friends used to call it) that the weed gives you after the first couple of pulls. That feeling took me to another world. I loved it.

After that I started to smoke daily and do stupid stuff with the crew. We'd pick on other kids and run from the police. Sometimes it felt good to be reckless with them. I liked the excitement. And hurting others seemed to get my own pain off my shoulders. It still hurt to be away from my family, and I felt alone, even when I was with my crew. No friends of mine could give me the love that I'd left behind in Russia.

When I chilled with the crew we looked like a gang and lots

of people were scared of us. Sometimes I didn't like that, because I didn't feel like myself. But it made me feel safe on the streets. After a while, I didn't feel scared of anything.

My mom could see the crew was a bad influence and tried her best to prevent me from hanging out with them. She would lock me inside the house, or find other things for me to do after school like swimming or a soccer team. At first I listened and did everything that she asked me to do.

But as time went on I started to get bored, and I didn't feel like following my mom's rules anymore. It was fun being stupid and not caring about anything. For the first time of my life, I was a badass.

Besides, being high all the time stopped me from thinking too much. I stopped worrying about my mom, and every time I smoked weed I would remember my family in Russia less and less.

One day my mom caught me smoking a cigarette and humiliated me right in front of my friends. First she slapped the cigarette out my hands and then she started to yell at me. I didn't know whether to be mad at myself for not listening to my mom or at her for humiliating me in front of my friends like that. I decided to be mad at her.

Sometimes it felt good to be reckless. I liked the excitement.

I started coming home very late, and sometimes not coming home at all. My mother kept on giving me punishments, but they weren't affecting my behavior. I wasn't a little kid who was scared to get hit with a belt anymore. I started to steal money from my mother to get more weed.

I loved my mom with all my heart, and stealing from her felt like stealing from myself. It hurt. But when I bought and smoked weed with the money that I stole, the pain went away. That cycle continued. My relationship with my mother started to fade, while my relationship with my friends got stronger.

In Russia my life was peaceful, and I had always been the

"perfect" child. But now I was getting into lots of fights and stealing stuff on a regular basis. Smoking weed didn't seem like the problem. The real problem was getting money.

One of my friends and I started stealing collector cards from Toys "R" Us and selling them on eBay. I'd never stolen that much before, and for the first time something inside of me told me that stealing wasn't the right thing to do. I wasn't used to that feeling. But since I really needed the money, I didn't let it bother me.

I started to steal more and more. Then one day I stole about $95 worth of cards and got caught. I started to cry because I thought it was the end of the world. I'd never in my life been handcuffed in a police car. I was terrified at the thought of going to jail.

Being high all the time stopped me from thinking too much. Every time I smoked weed I would remember my family in Russia less and less.

When my mom picked me up from the precinct she looked so depressed. I didn't know what to say. I thought she was going to yell at me and give me lots of punishments. But she wasn't saying anything to me at all. She was just looking out the window, and I could see on her face that she was thinking very hard about something.

After we got home I told her that I was really sorry, and that my punishment should be very big. But she told me there wasn't going to be a punishment. "I'm not going to punish you because you are old enough to control yourself and to think about your life," she said. "You are 14 years old, getting locked up and smoking weed."

For some reason I couldn't get those words out of my head: "You are old enough." What did that mean? Was I becoming older and maturing? Was I supposed to know how to survive by myself?

"It's like I'm becoming this monster," I thought to myself. "My mom looks so stressed. It looks like she's going through more pain than me." I felt like everything started to change against me. My shoulders felt very heavy, and my conscience started to burn me alive.

I wish I could say that was the day I started to straighten my life out. But it was just the beginning of the bad side of my life.

It would take me about two years to come back to this world and find the real me that I'd been looking for for years. I would never be that same perfect kid from Russia, but I found out how to be someone who feels good about himself and the life he's living in.

That night, I was really thinking about the person I had become, and how I wanted to change. But the next day I was too depressed to think about anything. So I dealt with it the way I always did—I got some weed, and got my mind out of this world.

Daniel was 17 and in high school when he wrote this story.

Gary Smith / YC Art Dept.

Losing My Life to Drugs

By Anonymous

I've been a serious drug abuser for more than three years of my life. My drug use started in my freshman year of high school as innocent curiosity. But now I can't remember months of my life because, at one point, the drugs completely took over. I get sad thinking about it.

Before using drugs, I'd seen TV commercials saying, "Don't do dope!" or "This is your brain on drugs," while showing an egg frying. I said to myself I'd never take drugs because the frying egg commercial scared me. I thought that the heat generated from drugs could actually fry your brain.

There were also drug prevention programs in junior high school, like SPARK. (SPARK stands for Support, Prevention, Awareness, Responsibility, and Knowledge.) Representatives talked to my health class about how drugs can mess you up. I was amazed at the things they showed us, all those pipes and bottles and bags of assorted contraband.

Yet even though drugs were scary, I still found myself wondering how it would feel to be on them.

By my freshman year in high school, I found out. Many kids at my school were doing drugs. The group I hung out with was especially into pot, LSD (acid), and ecstasy. But they didn't pressure me into taking anything. My own curiosity got the better of me.

One day I went with my friends to the field in back of my school. Somebody lit a joint. Everyone started taking puffs, but when it was my turn someone said, "Mike doesn't smoke."

"I want to try," I said. So I took a few pulls off it. I waited to get high, as I watched my friends feel the joint's effects. They were red-eyed and slow-moving. They talked about bananas. But I felt nothing. I said, "That's it? That's what everyone makes a big deal about?" I thought that maybe smoking pot just didn't have any effect on me.

I began to miss out on parts of my life because I couldn't remember certain things when I was high.

Days later, a student in school tried to sell me some LSD. It sounded very appealing to me because he said I'd slip into another dimension of sight and hearing. (Dude sounded like he was from the Twilight Zone.) But I turned him down because I wasn't sure about its negative effects.

But I didn't turn down pot. I thought weed was cool because a lot of people were doing it and I thought, "Hey, I didn't feel any different the first time. Why should it matter?"

The second time I smoked weed I was in my school's parking lot. I took the same number of pulls I'd taken the first time, but this time I got very high. I can't remember much past the first 15 minutes of being under the influence, but I do remember noticing things that I was oblivious to before, like the way the tiles in the school bathrooms were arranged—three gray tiles with a black tile in the middle.

I liked the feeling and smoked every day for three weeks straight. The bad thing was I felt tired and drained after the highs. And I began to miss out on parts of my life because I couldn't remember certain things while I was high.

Then I decided to buy LSD from the same dealer in my school. I wanted to try something different since I was growing bored with getting high from marijuana.

Actually, I was pretty bored with most of my life. I was doing fine in school and had hobbies like chess and soccer, but these things were just there to me. I was more excited by the new outlet drugs provided. So when it came time to take acid, which was on a little square piece of paper, I said to myself, "It can't possibly be that bad." So I took it and went on the strangest journey of my life. Weird ideas ran through my head. I thought about everything from deep meaningful questions like, "What do I want to do with my life?" to straight-up absurdities like, "What if I put a cat in a freezer?"

I was pretty bored with most of my life. I was doing fine in school and had hobbies, but I was more excited by the new outlet drugs provided.

As crazy as I felt under acid's influence, I wanted to do it again because I thought it was fun to go on that trip. But I didn't realize how many problems I'd have to deal with because of my LSD use. At home, even when I wasn't on it, I had flashbacks, which meant that I relived some of the craziness I experienced when I was tripping on acid. I also had random fits of panic and became very argumentative. The flashbacks were terrible; I hated not being in control while they happened.

One time I was doing my homework and then, in a second, I was consumed with fear because I couldn't figure out where the cat was. (I didn't have a cat.) Another day I was making breakfast and caught a flashback. Two minutes later, I was having a conversation with the toaster.

My mom started to wonder why I was acting so strangely. She didn't suspect I was taking LSD though. She asked me, "Mike, are you using marijuana?" in that classic parent finger-wagging tone.

"Of course not," I replied, even though my eyes were red and sweat was trickling down the side of my head.

By then I was taking acid several times a month. But one day, after taking acid at a party, I tripped out way too hard. Normally I took a tiny square piece. But the person I bought it from didn't cut his sheet and just ripped an unmeasured piece off, so I ended up taking a lot more than I was used to. I tripped so hard I couldn't talk straight. On the subway ride home, the horrible noise sounded like music to me. I came home at 3 o'clock in the morning hoping my mom wasn't waiting up. But she was. And she knew something was up. She asked me flat out what I'd taken. I admitted what I'd done.

She seemed very calm on the surface, but I knew she was distraught. She looked like she wanted to cry and her voice was high-pitched, which happens whenever she gets upset. I didn't want to see her like this.

She wanted to send me away to a rehab program but I wasn't having it. I'd miss the city too much. I pleaded with her for another alternative. I found an outpatient program in the city and she agreed to let me stay home if I checked myself into it. I had to go to the program at least twice a week and take a drug test once a month. If the test came back positive, I would've been sent to a detention center by the program. So I stayed sober for almost a year.

I participated in group sessions where we'd talk about how drugs negatively affected our lives. It was strange being the only kid in the group who'd done LSD. The other kids were there for smoking pot. The conversations were almost always about marijuana, which I'd stopped doing after I started tripping. So I kind of felt left out.

But one of my counselors could relate to my experiences. He told me that he used to drop so much acid in his day that when he caught flashbacks, he put his hand through store windows. And he took so many pills and drank so much that he found himself in strange positions and places in the morning. He also told the group that until we reached absolute rock bottom, we weren't ready to be rehabilitated.

Even though my counselor was probably trying to steer us away from making the same mistakes he had, I thought he was bragging in a way. So his stories rolled right off my back.

While I was in the program, the situation at home was tense. I had to be careful of everything I said and did so my mom wouldn't think I was doing drugs again. I wanted her to trust me. I also kept to myself a lot. Part of the rehab regimen was that I couldn't talk to my old friends anymore because you're supposed to move on from the past. I missed them and felt bored.

After nine months I was released from the program. I guess I hadn't hit my rock bottom yet because soon after my release, I started to sniff Special K, aka ketamine, which I bought from a school dealer. I also began popping prescription pills and drinking. That was probably worse than what I was doing before because a lot of prescription medications aren't supposed to be mixed with alcohol. It could've been fatal.

I got so drunk sometimes that I passed out in the street, like my counselor had. There were times I woke up with ashes in my mouth and paint or bloodstains on my clothes. For around six months, this was my life.

I think I got into drugs again to escape the real world. I was having trouble with my girlfriend, Danielle, and felt depressed about our relationship. She often lied to me about her whereabouts and cheated on me at least three times. I felt depressed and sad.

I found myself doing more and more drugs to escape emotional pain. But the mood swings and physical pain made me

Losing My Life to Drugs

wonder whether it was worth it. I was getting intense stomach-aches. After describing the pain to one of my female friends, she said, "It sounds a lot like when I get cramps."

Then, I ended up getting caught again. My mom was going through my pants pocket and found my bottle of pills. There was no other way to explain it but the truth. Luckily, she didn't send me upstate. Being caught again calmed me down a lot and I remained sober for three months. But even the fear of getting sent away didn't stop me from trying yet another drug, ecstasy. To me it was the ultimate high.

Starting in the summer, I took E as often as I could. When I was high, I felt like I was walking on air and my sensory perceptions increased tenfold. One trip consisted of me rubbing my body for an extended peri-od of time. But I was irritable and mean after my highs. I was hurting people around me, like my mom and new girlfriend, Veronica. (I'd broken up with Danielle.) When I was high,

I wanted to ask for help, but after disappointing my loved ones, I couldn't. I didn't want to hear "I told you so."

Veronica sometimes told me that I was acting crazy. I used to fight with her over the smallest things.

I once asked her, "How was your day?"

"Ugh!" she said.

"What the hell type of answer is that?" I yelled. Then we started to fight.

And my body felt even more wrecked. I used to get stomach cramps and chest pains that hurt so badly that I doubled over. My life had become messy and painful. One evening, I was doing homework on the floor at the side of my bed and was hit with a really bad cramp that stayed with me for five minutes. I closed my eyes and bent over in intense pain. My stomach felt like someone was violently twisting and pinching it from the inside. I thought, "I have to stop doing drugs."

The pain became my rock bottom. I realized that I had a major problem. I was tired of not being able to focus and of seeing my family upset. I was tired of the sleepless nights and not knowing where I was. And I couldn't endure the stomach cramps.

But most of all, I just didn't want to be a drug addict. I wanted to ask for help, but after disappointing my loved ones, I couldn't. I didn't want to hear "I told you so" or "Why didn't you listen?" I didn't want to go through the long, drawn-out emotional routine.

So I decided to stop cold turkey. The next day I got out of bed with a headache and dry mouth. For three days I went into withdrawal, which is how your body reacts to being taken off drugs that it's been given regularly. I had cold sweats, a fever, and diarrhea. Even though I felt terrible, I still went to school because I didn't want to mess up again.

In the four months since I stopped taking abusive substances, I've felt more determined to succeed. Once I hit rock bottom, all that I'd heard in the rehab program started to make sense. Instead of wanting to take drugs, I needed something more. I needed some type of control over my life again.

I started to chase my former goals again. And I stopped fighting with my family and girlfriend. I feel more at ease in the house, even though I still have to watch what I say because my parents might think I'm tripping out. They don't realize that I'm naturally crazy even when I'm not high.

Veronica also helps to keep me clean. She gets upset at the prospect of me doing drugs again; when I mention them she gives me a look. Plus, she doesn't put me through any strife, which means I'm not tempted to do drugs to escape emotional pain from my girlfriend.

But I hate when someone tells me they know what I've gone through when they've never done drugs before. I look them dead in the face and tell them "No, you don't." And when I look at people who do drugs now, it turns my stomach because I do know what it's like. I feel sorry for them.

It's hard not being able to recall parts of my life because of drugs. Some of my memory's so cloudy. Every time I try to remember certain things and can't, I feel like crying.

Staying drug-free isn't easy since I still know of many places to get drugs. I'm not sure how I'm going to stay clean, so I take it one day at a time. I try to place myself in fewer situations where drugs are available. And if someone offers me drugs, I find myself quickly saying, "No thanks," and head in the opposite direction. I think I got it down this time.

The writer was 18 when he wrote this story.
He went on to graduate high school.

Remy Whitacre

My Real Reasons
for Quitting Weed

By X. Reyes

When I was 13, I was having a lot of problems with my adoptive mother. She was abusing me and I stole things from her to get revenge. It got so bad that I ran away from home and lived on the streets for three months.

During those three months I started smoking weed. I did it to get my mind off all the troubles I had. And since I had a lot of troubles, I smoked a lot of weed. Sometimes I smoked weed with my crew, other times I smoked it by myself. I usually got high after the first blunt, but if I didn't, then two more afterwards did the trick.

Every time I got high, I would go through the same stages of reliving memories. Some of these memories were very violent, while others were calm and quiet. For example, I always got very quiet after I smoked my first blunt. I'd sit down and think about the times that my adoptive mother abused me and called me "N-gger lover," "Negro," and "black boy" just because I had black friends.

As I remembered her verbal abuse, my anger would begin to build up. I'd get mad and become very violent because the weed made these memories so vivid, as if the abuse happened yesterday. I got so angry that I'd call people names and try to fight them if they answered back.

"Hey, you got the time?" I once asked this guy when I was high.

"No," the guy said. He just kept walking.

"You know why you ain't got the time? 'Cause you too damn poor to buy a watch. You be spending all that damn money on crack for you and your ho!"

The guy stopped and looked at me like I was crazy.

"Don't say anything about my wife!" he screamed.

I smoked weed to get my mind off all my troubles. And since I had a lot of troubles, I smoked a lot of weed.

"Shut the @#%& up! You know something? Your wife is just like a doorknob, everyone gets a turn!"

"What did you say?" he asked as he came toward me.

"Chill!" all of my homies said. They jumped in front of him and told him that I was crazy. I was in the back, yelling at them to let him fight me, but my homies made the guy walk away.

After that I'd run around, knock over garbage cans, and chase cats into the street so they'd get hit by cars. This stage lasted about two hours. Then, just as the high was ending, I would enter a stage where I felt depressed and guilty. I'd blame myself for getting abused. I'd cry until all my tears were gone. Then I would wipe my eyes, get high again, and go through the same moods all over again.

Fun, isn't it?

By getting high, I was only trying to block out all the pain that I felt from living on the streets. But the only thing that smoking weed did was bring back bad memories from the past. Instead of blocking out the pain, it only made it worse.

After I entered the foster care system I kept on with my weed smoking. I didn't want the bad memories to disrupt my pleasant high. But no matter what I did, I couldn't stop the memories of my gloomy childhood. A childhood filled with abuse, neglect, and racism from my adoptive mother. Nights when I went to bed without food or water, days when my adoptive mother made me wear the same clothes over and over without changing them. Memories that haunted me every time I'd get high.

I felt so tortured that I decided there was only one way out— to quit smoking. The high was excellent, but if giving it up meant that the horrible memories wouldn't haunt me, then I figured I could live without it.

The only thing that smoking weed did was bring back bad memories from the past. Instead of blocking out the pain, it made it worse.

It took a lot of patience to quit. I was really addicted. It was like Mike Tyson giving up boxing. Day after day I'd try to think of something to do to help me quit. The craving was unbearable. It was like finding a million dollars on the street and then having to give it back.

Sometimes when I felt like getting high, I'd go to sleep or eat a lot. Other times I'd take long walks. Then I got a new girl, so I was able to take my mind off weed. I stopped hanging out with the people who smoked weed. There were times when I wanted to smoke so badly that I would've been willing to offer any amount of money to someone to get it for me. But I knew that I had to stop if I wanted the memories to stop.

After about seven weeks of suffering, the craving finally disappeared. It seemed like it happened overnight. One day I was dying to smoke; the next morning I couldn't even stand thinking about it. I finally realized that ganja hadn't done anything for me but put me through seven weeks of pure hell.

I quit two years ago and haven't picked up a blunt since. Every time someone offered me one I'd refuse, because I knew that my nightmare would start all over again.

So you see, there's another reason why people stop smoking weed, other then getting busted or because of what it physically does to their bodies. Nobody ever talks about the inner feelings they have when they smoke weed. No one ever talks about the bad memories or feeling paranoid or guilty. If they did, they would come to understand that smoking weed doesn't make their pain go away. It only makes it come back twice as hard.

The writer was 17 when he wrote this story. He went on to graduate from college and is now a project manager at a major media company.

Ed Marquez III

Interviews With Dealers: Taking Care of Business?

By Anonymous

"As long as there ain't another way to feed my family, I'll be selling drugs."

"I ain't here to hurt nobody, I'm just trying to make a living."

Around my block, drug dealing is a major problem. I live in Harlem, in New York City. It's hard to walk down the streets near Broadway without being hassled by drug dealers or crackheads.

To look into this problem, I went out and interviewed teens and adults in the community about drugs and why people deal them.

One of the main reasons why people deal, or think about dealing, is because of the money. Even teenagers who don't deal say they understand the temptations. Pebbles, a 15-year-old from Manhattan, said she thought about dealing because "I needed the money." She believes that little kids see the drug dealers getting mad money and expensive cars, so they think: "Why go to school when I could be dealing?"

Lillian, a 17-year-old from Brooklyn, New York, agrees with Pebbles. She said that it's like a chain effect. "Young people see old people doing it, so they gonna do it." She said that's the way she started smoking weed. Her friends did it, so she did it too. She quit smoking when her best friend died of leukemia.

In fact, most of the teenagers I interviewed admitted they used marijuana. Pebbles told me that she smokes weed because it relaxes her nerves. Manny, a 19-year-old from Manhattan, said that he never used drugs, but admitted that he smokes marijuana. He said weed isn't a drug, "it's a medicine."

It wouldn't have been fair to just talk to teens and grownups, so I took the risk of talking to drug dealers as well. So many lives are being ruined because of drugs, and way too many kids are going into foster care because their parents use drugs and can't take care of them. How can anyone who knows this deal drugs during the day and still sleep at night?

I was surprised at what I found. In some ways, drug dealers think they are no different from us. They say they are simply trying to make a living. They say they aren't trying to hurt anyone, that they're just doing what they have to do to survive.

Most drug dealers admitted that they sold weed to teenagers. I asked "Number One," a drug dealer, why he sold drugs to teenagers. He said, "This is my job. I ain't gonna tell them 'no.' This is business."

For many, dealing is the easiest and fastest job that doesn't require an education or experience. Drug dealers said they make lots of money. At least, more than you'd make "in a regular job. Unless you a lawyer or something," said Dibs, a 19-year-old dealer from Manhattan.

Number One is a 20-year-old family man. He lives with his 3-year-old son and his girlfriend. He also supports his mother, because his dad was never around. He told me that his dad has been in jail as long as he can remember.

His mother knows he deals. She doesn't like it, but like Number One said, "My moms doesn't approve, but I gots to do it anyways." He deals because that's the way he supports his family.

Number One dropped out of school when he was 15. "I just wanted to chill with my friends," he said. "You know, smoke weed and play hooky all day long." He was 18 when he started dealing. He said he had to act fast because his girl had gotten pregnant and he had to take on responsibilities.

His girlfriend, Janice, is only 17. She's still in high school and is going to college next year. Janice is aware that her man is a hustler. Her mother knows, too. Janice told me her mom didn't agree with Number One selling drugs, but her mom also knew he wasn't a bad kid. "She knew him since he was born," Janice said.

All the money and the expensive gear only blinds our eyes and hides the truth: "There are only two ways out—either you end up dead or in jail."

Janice told me that things are hard, that it's not easy to make a living without an education. It's hard enough for people who have legal jobs. Both Janice and Number One felt too young to take on the responsibilities of being a parent. "I got pregnant, we both young," Janice said. "What was he supposed to do? At least he didn't walk out on me, like most n-ggas be doing."

Of drug dealing, she said, "It's not that it's right or anything. It's just the way to maintain a living." She believes that if Number One hadn't left school, he wouldn't be dealing. She said this about drug dealers in general: "They blew their opportunity away by not going to school."

Number One admits that when his girl got pregnant, he didn't try to look for a legal job because "it takes mad time to go out and look for a job. I needed to act fast. I needed to move my girl in. This is like the fastest thing to do. Not the smartest, but hey," he said in a high-pitched tone, looking frustrated and throwing his hands high in the air.

Most teenagers said that there are jobs out there, but getting them takes work. Still, they didn't think that the difficulty of getting a job should be an excuse to sell.

"If you do submit to selling drugs, it's like you're giving up," said 15-year-old Pebbles.

Many of the people I talked to felt the same way. A lot of kids are in the foster care system because of drug abuse in their families. Little kids in the street are looking at the drug market for role models.

"There's already a lot of people out there who are sick, and crackheads and bums," said 17-year-old Lillian. There's "homeless who don't have money, but be buying crack. [Dealers] try to make money but they destroying families."

The drug dealers, however, insist that they need to make a living and make other excuses.

"I love my son, and I wouldn't like him to sell or use this stuff," said Number One. "But then again, this is what kids see as they grow up. I know this is what I grew up seeing."

Some of the people I interviewed said that most of the drug dealers are illegal immigrants or don't have other ways of making a living. "If I don't put food in my house, who will?" asked Number One, who agrees with Dibs, the 19-year-old dealer from Manhattan, that it's just a way of survival.

Maybe if the drug dealers could survive with a little less stuff, they could find a less destructive line of work. When I walk around my neighborhood, I see all these drug dealers dressed mad fly. So it makes me think. We all like expensive stuff nowadays. In fact, most of the teens interviewed said easy money was the real problem.

"It's hard to admit it, but our world is too materialistic. I am too," said Janice. She lives in a fly four-bedroom apartment, and has a big screen TV in her room hooked to a cable box, a DVD player, and a video game player. A computer is right next to her bed, and she has a closet full of the latest fashions. But the toddler's room amazed me the most.

"Little Number One" has a room of his own. Even though he sleeps with his parents, they prepared a little room for him for when he gets older. He has a closet full of name brand clothes. His sneakers range from the latest Jordans and Nike Airs to the oldest styles. He has his own TV, also hooked to a cable box and DVD player, a boom box, and a CD player. He also has a big cabinet full of toys. His room has Looney Toons and Disney characters on the walls along with a framed photograph of his first birthday with his mom and dad.

My own cousin Jason (who I consider my brother) owns a BMW and dresses better than all of his friends. His wife is well maintained. My nephew has all the Jordans, a phat chain and expensive gear. The reason they have all this is because Jason is a drug dealer.

This sounds good, right?

Truth is, it isn't. My cousin got arrested last summer. The sad part is that my nephew saw the cops take his daddy. My nephew is only 2 years old, but he is smart. Jason's wife is pregnant right now. My family is destroyed. My aunts and my mom don't stop crying. I can't help but cry too. My nephew is constantly asking where his daddy is. He isn't used to sleeping without him.

Jason isn't a bad kid. Jason was a real smart kid in high school. He was an honor roll student and he played football. He was going to go to UCLA, but he left school before graduating. He's 22 years old. His wife is 24, and just graduated with a computer degree.

Through selling drugs, Jason took care of his mom, brothers and sister, his wife, his kid, and even me. With no father around, he felt responsible for the whole family.

But it all backfired when a guy from my block snitched on him. Sooner or later you pay the consequences. Money can't buy happiness. It isn't living large.

An education can give you real happiness. Getting a career might seem impossible, 'cause it takes a lot of hard work and time, but in the end it pays off. You'll always have it, you won't be put in jail for it, you can be proud of it, and you'll be successful for the rest of your life. And it won't hurt anyone.

The drug business is not an easy way out. It doesn't last a lifetime. Anything that comes easy, goes away easy. Don't settle for less, and don't let appearances fool you. All the money and the expensive gear only blinds our eyes and hides the truth.

As Manny, a 19-year-old from Manhattan put it, "There are only two ways out—either you end up dead, or in jail."

As I write this, my cousin's still in jail.

The writer was 18 and in high school when
she wrote this story.

Melanie Leong

My So-Called Holidays

By Sidney Black

I don't really celebrate holidays. It's not because I'm a Jehovah's Witness. It's because I'm in the foster care system. And the system's the place where every holiday seems the same: a bottle and a blunt!

Those of you in the system probably know what it's like to share every birthday with people you've only known for a couple of months. And then there's the family situation.

How about the tale of the forgetful mother, my mother, who didn't remember what day it was when her own son called to thank her for giving him life? At least I got a good cake a week later, when my group home finally realized they had missed the day. On my actual birthday, I only had my good old pals, a bottle and a blunt, to keep me company.

Or how about the time I was banned from my family's

Christmas dinner? My grandmother was mad at me for arguing with my moms. They said I was free to leave, or else I had to stay on the top floor of my house.

Everyone came to visit. Aunts and uncles I hadn't seen in years. Yeah, I saw them—out my window, while I was getting drunk.

It's funny how the weed spots stay open all Christmas Day. So when my family began to feast, I went to the store, found my boy Young, picked up my boys Garcia, Vega, and Chocolate, and we had our own last supper (minus the food). I still got a plate of fixings from my moms when it was over. I was just too drunk to enjoy it.

On my birthday, I only had my good old pals, a bottle and a blunt, to keep me company.

These are just some of the reasons why, whatever the holiday, I won't be celebrating. To understand more fully, let's see what the holidays mean to me one by one.

New Year's Eve: A day when everybody who is quiet as hell goes to Times Square to be cold, loud, and drunk. For some reason, I usually end up in some type of trouble. One time I ended up with the highest THC level, and my group home sent me on a trip to rehab. But at least I got a free vacation to ring in the New Year, right?

Valentine's Day: How much love am I feeling when the only people I see are paid to watch me? So you probably know by now where I turn looking for love.

Good Friday: For me Good Friday doesn't come around just once a year. I celebrated Good Friday every Friday for the past two years. Only the palms and oils I used were weed and Bacardi. So you know I saw the Holy Ghost! But this time it was the pastor who sent my ass to rehab.

Mother's Day: She's tried to kill me at least five times. Should she still get a card?

Father's Day: I remember every time I got beat for no reason, but he's changed now. He's the perfect father—to his new kids, that is.

Independence Day: It was my first holiday in the system and just because I was contained to one floor doesn't mean I wasn't glad to see the fireworks of freedom…on TV.

Thanksgiving: My family all gathers. I may or may not be there. I feel uncomfortable around people I've known all my life when we still don't know a thing about each other. I wait till it's over and either get drunk, high, or drunk and high to help me deal with feeling out of place with my own family.

Christmas: Thanksgiving times two. But at least last year Santa brought me a bottle of Smirnoff, Bacardi Gold, and some kosher grape wine. Thanks, Santa!

I'm so sick of people telling me to cheer up, it's such and such day. Just give me a bottle, some sweet potato pie and trust me, the holiday won't be wasted.

P.S. Don't do drugs.

Sidney (not his real name) was 19 when he wrote this story.
He served in the Marines, and now runs his own
tech company.

Percyell Smith

Smoke and Mirrors

By Anonymous

When I started smoking weed, it made me feel comforted. I could express how I felt and talk to people I barely spoke to normally. Weed brought out a side of me I liked—loud, outspoken, and yet calmer about things. Usually, I get angry pretty quick, but when I was high, nothing bothered me. Being high felt like my friend, because as long as I stayed high, everything was all right.

When I first started, I didn't worry about how much I liked getting high. I thought, "It's just on the weekends." Then smoking became something I had to do. As time went by, I began to see that the way I carried myself and my whole attitude with people changed.

My appearance changed too because I always had the urge to eat after getting high. I gained weight and didn't take care of the way I looked. After a while, I also noticed that the friends I smoked with weren't really my friends.

Once I went to my favorite block in Harlem to smoke some chocolate (weed) with my friends. I was chillin' until I started feeling hot and like my heart was beating fast. I told them, "I need air," because I felt nauseous. They started to panic because they were so high. I was thinking, "I am going to die with these high dummies."

Eventually I threw up, and after that, my friends didn't want to hang out with me anymore. That would have upset me before, but at that point I really didn't care that they didn't stand by me. That made me realize how much I'd changed.

Even before I got into weed, living with my mom was never easy. She's tough on me. My mother got pregnant by a drug addict who physically abused her. Maybe that's why she's hard on me, to protect me from the same things happening to me, but I don't really know.

My mom is a single parent who works hard, and she is very religious. She's always at work or school or church. She was never there to give love. I always felt uncomfortable around her, like we were strangers.

I felt like it was a waste of time to tell my mother how I felt. Often she told me, "Don't say anything." That made me feel alone.

As I kept smoking, my relationship with my mom got more difficult, because everything I did involved weed, not spending time with her. And I would straight disrespect her.

She also crossed the line between tough love and abuse. When we got in physical fights, it took me a long time to say to myself, "This is abuse." She beat me up once because I ate three pieces of chicken. She also criticized me constantly about my weight, which I could never understand. I'd say, "You the same size as I am." But she didn't want to hear it.

Another time we were fighting, really fighting, and she bit me on my finger. I was like, "What are you doing?" But she just called the cops and told them I started it. She played like everything was my fault.

I had all this hatred inside me, and confusion. I didn't understand—why were things like this? Sometimes I'd feel angry to the point that I really wanted to stab her. She made me feel so much pain. Why shouldn't she feel the pain, too?

When I thought like that, I tried to forget it. I felt like it was a waste of time to tell my mother how I felt. Often she told me, "Don't say anything." That made me feel alone.

When she noticed I was smoking weed, my mother saw me following my father's footsteps. But I ignored my mother's warnings about becoming a drug addict, because it's hard to respect someone who doesn't show it back. Instead, I started hanging out late, doing drugs, and cutting school. I stayed away from home for weeks at a time and depended on everyone else for love.

At first I felt independent, because I could do exactly what I wanted. But other times, when I was high, my mind just raced and I couldn't control my emotions. I didn't know how I was feeling and I didn't know how to respond to things.

I felt scared of what was happening to me. Sometimes I would cry because I would wonder, "Why me and not someone else?" I felt low about myself, like I didn't know who I was anymore.

Eventually, the high from weed wasn't as strong anymore and I wanted to try other drugs. Plus, when I wasn't high, it was harder for me to concentrate, and sometimes I wouldn't feel like myself when the high went down. I had to admit that I had a problem with weed.

Finally, my mother put me in foster care because she couldn't control me. Being in the system gave me a big break from the street, but I hated the rules and taking urine tests every weekend after my home visit. I was given several chances to get myself together, to prove that I was in control of the drugs, not the other way around. But I wasn't in control.

I smoked on home visits anyway. I figured, "What can they do to me?" But soon I was placed in a drug treatment program.

Treatment helped me so much. I've realized now what caused me to do drugs. I felt alone and that made me turn to a drug for comfort. Before I went to treatment, nobody ever saw my side of the story. It was always, "She's doing this and that, hanging out with guys till 3 a.m. She's addicted to drugs." No one ever asked me any questions. They didn't try to know my side of the story—not in court, and not in the system.

In the program, they weren't so quick to judge. They didn't talk behind my back. They listened. I realized that I hold my feelings in, and that's what causes me to get out of control. I didn't know any other way to explain how I felt besides arguing, fighting, or doing disrespectful things to people.

Before I went to treatment, no one ever asked me any questions.

Since then, I've learned other ways to express myself. Now I express my feelings by writing to the person I'm upset with, talking to someone I feel comfortable with, and crying. I notice that after doing all these things I feel much better and even forget about what made me upset or angry.

I've also made some changes in my appearance that make me feel very good. And my attitude has changed from loud and disrespectful to quieter and more respectful. I can't say I'm perfect. Being in the system has not been easy, and I still AWOL (run away).

It doesn't help that my relationship with my mother is still a struggle. When she put me in the system, she started to act like she was trying to help me, but I feel like she's been less a supporter and more a critic. It seems like she's always blowing my addiction in my face. She puts me down and that makes me want to get high even more.

Now, when I act out, I feel like I'm getting back at her. When

I AWOL and my mother doesn't know where I am, I feel glad that I'm doing what I want to do and she can't stop me. Basically, when I'm running in the streets, it's to punish her. I love my mother, and I want things to work out, but I don't think it's going to happen that way.

The writer was 17 and in high school
when she wrote this story.

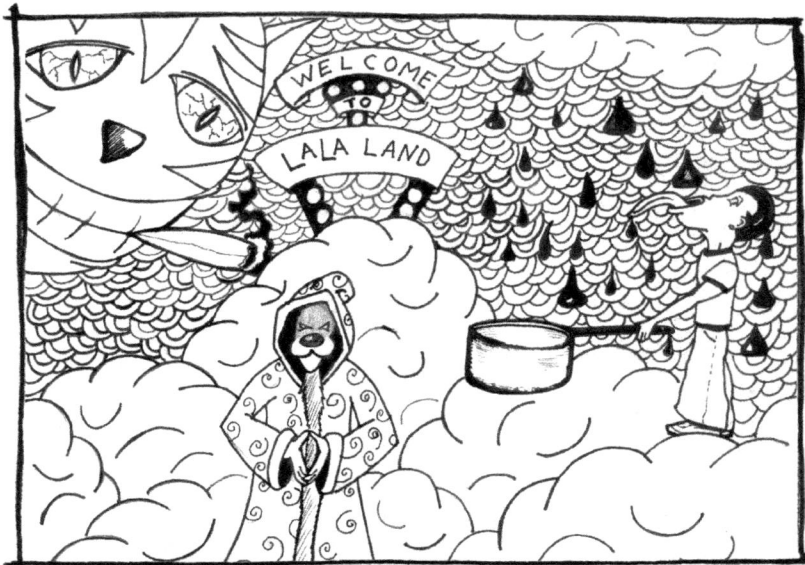

Fernando Quinones

How to Get to LaLa Land

By Anonymous

Lesson #1: Where to Smoke

Nighttime or daytime, when picking a smoking spot, make sure you're comfortable. My favorite spot is under the night sky watching the unblinking eyes.

If you like crowded places, make sure you hold the burning end in your palm and keep your eyes open. If the cops still catch you with your eyes glazed over and painted pretty red, be as pleasant as possible. That way you can give the impression of "a good kid who does bad things." This gets sympathy on your side. If you have a nasty attitude toward the cops, they'll mark you as one of the local hoods and make your record book so thick with any little petty thing you do that they'll need a briefcase for all your papers.

For the real bold, put the fan backward in the window after your parents are snoring and blow wisps of smoke through the dim light of your favorite scented candle. Have fun watching the smoke form into your innermost desires. Dispose of the ashes and roaches out the window. To be sure you won't start any fires, smash them up real good in your makeshift ashtray.

Lesson #2: Choosing a Smoking Partner

When choosing smoking partners, choose wisely, because not everyone agrees that sparking up is a good escape from the stress you endure daily, though they have no idea what you go through and show no attempt to understand you. (That's no big deal, because the lovable Mary J will understand every complex piece of you.)

No, stick to your own kind, someone who can understand your need to light up. And find someone to smoke with who'll

When you return from LaLa Land your problems are still there, in a pile of rubble unsolved

take care of you if you feel like getting bent out of your mind and taking a trip to LaLa Land. Don't be ashamed to have a fellow puffer on hand in case you start seeing talking dogs or feel like flying off from the highest point in the city and wind up falling on your ass.

But it's difficult to know just whom you can trust. Your friend might steal your money or have a moment of passion with you or spread your secret recipe. So alternate the times when you take care of him and when he takes care of you. That way everyone gets a bent turn, and you secure your memories of his stupid times, which you can use as blackmail if you need to.

Lesson #3: What to Do in Your Daze

Now, what to do after you're in the cloud of daze, that's up to you. Some people find it perfectly normal to go about their lives as if they haven't even touched Mary J. Sparking up before they join the real world gives them an extra boost of confidence or tolerance to stomp through and make waves.

Sure, it might mess you up when it comes to your job or schoolwork. Like when I was high in math class, I rarely paid attention. Instead, I drew pictures of clouds and wrote poetry about how frustrating math was and how much I wanted to stab the teacher in the eye. (No, I didn't pass.)

But that's OK, because with a little help from the weed, I more than made up for it with a stellar performance in English class. I gave the whole class stomachaches from laughing with my over-imaginative answers, such as, "Of course, Romeo wanted to hit that. Why do you think he was going up to Juliet's balcony like that? To get in."

It can seem like the world is slowing down. It's not, though. It's just that you're stuck in a rut going in circles.

Now at home, that's a different story. It can cause quite a little bit of havoc with your family. Before I started smoking, I was pretty much a "yes ma'am" kind of girl. But after, I started whistling a different tune.

I would ignore my grandmother's rules about being home, hence I would not be home. When I finally did come in and she'd reprimand me, I'd slam my bedroom door in her face and pump my radio so loud you could hear it from the lobby of my apartment building. This was also against her rules.

She'd push the door open and yell some more about respecting her under her roof. All I would do is give her a wide smile and start talking philosophical. "You know you're not supposed to dwell on the negative because that's what causes stress." Believe me, she really hated my Mary J philosophizing.

But even at home, your habit can be a source of amusement. One time, I was getting ready for a party. I was so high on that cloud number nine that I gave my grandmother a hug. She sniffed me and said "Mmmm, what is that? It smells good?" Doh! I had completely forgotten that I smelled of nothing but pure weed.

I was about to make an excuse, but then she said, "Is it a new shampoo or perfume?"

"Yeah, it's a new Herbal Essence." I let go of her and quickly walked to my room. My friend and I had to put the radio loud to stifle our laughs from that one. To this day I giggle every time I think about it.

But in general, when you're high, stay away from home. I don't like anyone to blow my high, so I keep myself away from stress for as long as possible when I'm in my cloud. I don't want anyone to call me back from LaLa Land.

Lesson #4: Return from LaLa Land

LaLa Land. It might sound like some wonderful place where you can spaz out swallowing chocolate raindrops while you talk to the dog who has a master's degree in helping other people solve their problems. Where you lie on your back and watch the dark clouds and search for the moon to shine its cool light on you. Where the moon looks like a silver tooth in the Cheshire Cat's mouth. Where you feel like you're on a boat far off in the middle of the ocean, and it rocks you like a child rocks her body, for comfort. Where you can walk back to your home, where the drug dealers let you know that they have your supply, and you think, "Hey, those are my friends."

Well it is. But let me warn you, when you return from LaLa Land everything's not so dandy. When you return you might feel depressed that the dog wasn't real and that your problems are still there, in a pile of rubble, unsolved.

When you smoke, you let your imagination believe the things it conjures up are real, or at the very least possible. But somewhere in the back of your mind you're aware that, just like last time, you will have to come back down from these comfortable clouds. They dissipate slowly as the high wears away.

When you wake up from your daydreams, sometimes you think that ganja is perfectly good therapy. But most of the time you're just left with this headache that's caused by the very mode of transportation that took you on your trip. You miss the euphoric daze you had when you were in the clouds. You miss how it gave you that sense of being a child again, carefree. You miss how your heart lightened and you worried less about the loved ones you lost before you could show them how much you loved them. After, you feel even sadder than before.

And you do realize that being high, and numb to your pain, can be dangerous, too. Because you might not be able to feel the cold wind that blows up there on the highest points of the city, the warning that maybe you should back away from the edge or you might fall. Sometimes you can believe that if you're not aware of what's going on around you, the world will slow down. The world's not really slowing down, though. It's just that you're stuck in a rut going in circles. All the while, the world continues to spin on its pretty axis.

This realization leads you to find other ways to relieve this tension. You write, read, dance, sing, give advice to others while trying to solve your problems. You might even have sex. You don't have to kiss the blunt to feel good.

But you already did it once so you end up missing it, even though it left your mind in a haze. Eventually, you'll come across it one day and you'll be faced with the question, "To puff, or not to puff?" It's up to you.

The writer was 18 and in high school when she wrote this story. She went on to college.

YC Art Dept.

If You Trip, You Might Fall

By Anonymous

Two years ago, I was a naive 14-year-old who didn't even know what acid was, nor had I ever in my wildest dreams imagined what effect it could have on my mind. Sure, I'd smoked pot plenty of times, but there's no comparison between weed and LSD. I wish I had known then what I know now.

Every 4th of July my friends Angela and Judy and I go down to the river and watch the fireworks with our families. That year was special. Sam, a 20-year-old guy I had met in the park two days earlier, was going with us. Even though I had only known Sam a short time, I felt it had been years—an eternity. And even though I had no particular reason to, I trusted him.

Maybe that is why I smiled when, a couple of hours before the fireworks were supposed to start, he unfolded the shred of paper holding a half a tab of LSD and told me what it was. Sam said that if I slipped the tiny triangular piece of paper under my tongue, I would see fireworks even when I closed my eyes.

"What are you, nuts?" asked Judy when I hinted I might do it. "I wouldn't trust it if I were you," said Angela, planting a double meaning. What they were actually saying was: "You don't even know the guy, and you're gonna trust him enough to take drugs with him?"

I was curious: what did he mean, I'd see fireworks even when I closed my eyes? I decided to take the chance. I opened my mouth and let him drop the supposedly miraculous piece of paper under my tongue.

After that we all went to a local park that was fenced off and had signs that said "No Trespassing." I showed Sam around. I was in a great mood. Leaving the park, we had to climb over an old gate. On my way over, I seemed to get stuck for a moment. I tugged on my leg, but it wouldn't budge. Then I glanced at everyone else, their mouths opened in horror. Looking down at my leg, I realized I had caught it on razor wire. A jagged piece of metal was stuck in my leg, but I felt no pain.

I didn't know what to think, mainly because I had no idea what was going on. Was blood really rushing out of my leg? Judy and Angela stood there speechless. Sam told me that it was just a small cut and that I shouldn't look at it.

I was feeling no pain at all, not even when he bent down and pulled out the silver blade that was still lodged there. I just giggled, thinking the whole incident was hysterical. Sam insisted that I still not look at it, even though it was such a tiny cut. "It's mind over matter," he told me.

The four of us walked to Angela's house, where our parents were waiting for us. Nothing was too out of the ordinary. I just felt extra happy. "Not a bad drug," I thought. When we reached Angela's, the parents were sitting at the dining room table, talking and drinking coffee. I introduced Sam and we watched TV for a while.

It was about 8 p.m. Outside you could hear music blasting,

the rumble of fireworks, and occasionally loud laughter. Sam and I went outside to enjoy all the racket. We walked down the block and smoked a joint. Then things began to change.

Judy and Angela weren't with us and I remember thinking I should go upstairs and ask them to come outside. I missed them. But I was getting more and more confused. It was like I had forgotten how to go upstairs. So I just sat on the steps and watched the pretty colors flying through the air, wondering how much money the neighbors had spent on fireworks.

I was in my glory. The night air was warm on my skin and Sam and I were getting to know each other. He asked me to be his girlfriend.

Nine o'clock rolled around and we all started walking toward the river. Things started to look strange. The pavement seemed to become part of the river; waves formed in the concrete as if the tide were coming in. The light posts began to wiggle like they were dancing. It was hard to believe that such a tiny piece of paper could do all this. I was

Sam said that if I slipped the tiny paper under my tongue, I would see fireworks even when I closed my eyes.

finding it hard to even remember how to walk. The concrete tide was getting higher and higher. Was it going to swallow me?

I began to really freak out. I didn't know what normal was anymore, so I didn't know how I should act. My mind didn't feel right. I stopped talking, I figured that whatever came out of my mouth would be wrong, and everyone would know I was on some kind of drug. Whenever someone talked to me, I just smiled and pretended I was having fun.

When we all got to the river, the crowd was unbearable. I remember looking at Judy and Sam, and somehow they had exchanged eyes. Judy had Sam's eyes and Sam had Judy's. At that point I felt like I was going insane and I would never be the same.

My mother asked me if I wanted ice cream and I kept saying "What?" She started yelling at me, saying that I was embarrassed to eat ice cream in front of Sam. Something in my brain snapped at that moment and wouldn't allow me to comprehend what anyone was saying. I felt trapped.

We never got to see the fireworks. It seemed that we had arrived too late. We all headed toward the park, my mother giving Sam the third degree. I kept asking myself what was going on. I knew my mom was angry, but I couldn't understand why. I couldn't even stick up for Sam because I didn't know what my mother was saying. It sounded as if everyone was talking another language—gibberish.

I couldn't comprehend what anyone was saying. I felt trapped.

My mom was screaming at the top of her lungs now. Poor Sam, I was surprised he didn't just walk away. It seemed as if Sam started chanting, "Run with me, run with me." I took a last look at my hostile mother and, well, ran with him.

We walked for a while. I felt like I had just escaped from a mental hospital. Sam and I sat down by some factories. My nerves were like a set of electrical wires during a rainstorm.

"Relax and enjoy it," Sam said and smiled. I felt like he was my guardian angel. I was comprehending everything now, my "peak" was over. Then I heard my mother's voice calling my name. "She's here," I thought. I was staring at a garbage can. I told Sam and he said, "Trust me, your mom's not here. It's OK." He said "trust me" a million times and I finally gave in.

I calmed down and closed my eyes. I did see the fireworks that I had missed at the river. Sam and I talked on and on into the night. There was some kind of magic bond between us. I felt strangely safe with him. Thank God, because otherwise I think I would have literally been going crazy.

About 4 a.m., we decided to say goodnight. I wondered when I'd see Sam again. It had been one nutty night. I walked through the streets full of dead fireworks and liquor bottles. When I got home, my mom apologized for embarrassing the hell out of me.

Then she asked what had happened to my leg.

I looked down and suddenly realized that the "tiny" cut was really a huge gash. The blood actually glued my stockings onto me. And it didn't even hurt.

The next day, I remember feeling depressed, probably because the world was amazingly colorful and new when I was on the LSD and now it was back to the same old, dull world I knew before.

Looking back, in some ways I'm glad that I tried LSD, because it was an amazing experience. My first acid trip enabled me to see beyond reality and opened my mind. But I also know now just how dangerous it can be. I wish I had understood the effects of acid before I did it, that way maybe I would have been better prepared.

I now know that you shouldn't just take acid from anyone. God knows what it'll do to you and your body. I found out the hard way that tripping with my mom around is a no-no, for example. And if you're not comfortable where you are and who you're with, you are very likely to get paranoid and have a bad trip.

I also realize now that I freaked out because I thought it was me who was strange, when it was only the LSD. At the time, I didn't know it would go away in eight hours.

I still have a scar on my leg from that first acid trip and just thinking about it terrifies me. Something much, much worse could have happened to me. Even trusting Sam was incredibly dumb. He could've turned out to be a maniac and hurt me. Sam could have even left me alone, which would have been so frightening I might have really gone insane. My mind was so messed up back then that whatever he told me, I would have believed. You know the saying, "If he jumped off a roof, would you jump too?" Well, on LSD, I most likely would have.

Basically, I went into it blindly and that is the worst thing I could have done to myself. I've done acid a few more times after that because I wanted to enjoy it. But when I tried it again

I didn't feel totally in control. I was scared something would go wrong and I wouldn't be able to handle it. The thought of losing control scares me to the point where I can't have fun. If only acid weren't so intense.

Now that I am more aware of the dangers, I'm not sure if I will ever do it again. I'm at the point where I don't know whether or not it's really worth putting myself in such a dangerous situation.

The writer was in high school when she wrote this story.

Shamel Allison

A Fine Line Between Experimentation and Addiction

By Natasha Santos

As I was rushing out of the train station on my way to night school (a prison I attend twice a week because I'm one of those academic screw-ups that I never thought I'd be), I heard someone say "Ta–sha!!"

I turned around and saw my friend, Caleb. He's from Slovakia and has the most desirable Slavic accent. He's about 17, tall with blonde hair and blue eyes. He's smart and nice, reckless and just a little troubled. I admired that recklessness. Being around him made me feel alive. I wanted to be reckless and carefree and above all the consequences.

"You have to go get a drink," he told me as he rifled through his book bag.

"OK... Why?" I asked, a bit flustered.

"Because you have to take de pillzz," he said, producing a packet of cough medicine that you can buy at any drug store. Take enough of them, he said, and they send you on psychedelic trip lasting hours.

"Um, OK, I guess."

He had offered the pills to me before, but I'd only pretended to take them. Tonight, though, I was feeling adventurous. Taking the little pills out of the packets, my hands were shaking.

"When will they start working? What will happen?"

"You will feel like robot. Everything will be slow."

I dropped one. Purposely, I think. But he just picked it up.

"Eww! No way am I eating that. It has germs!" I said.

He placed it back into my hand alongside the others. "See, now you cannot tell which one it is."

I took a swig of water, put the pills in my mouth and waited for them to take effect. We walked around for a bit, skipping first period. "I'm starting to feel it," he said. "Do you feel anything?"

"Not yet. I hope it doesn't work," I said.

"It will work, it takes about an hour. You will feel it; you will like it." On our way back he threw up. "It is good. I like throwing up, because afterwards I feel it," he said. "I want a cigarette."

Thirty minutes later I felt tired, mellow. Everything was super slow. Turning my head made kaleidoscopes of colors that I couldn't decipher for minutes—or what felt like minutes. Every time I checked the clock only a minute or even just a few seconds had passed.

I spent the night at my friend's house. I didn't want my adoptive mother to see my dizzy face and ask questions. I was ashamed. I knew better. I had seen first-hand how drugs and addiction could destroy lives.

My biological mom had been addicted, and my dad had been a dealer. I had seen my mother go from being the somewhat normal, loving person that I had known through most of my formative years into a crazy, depressed, beaten, apathetic woman who refused to see the disorder, chaos, and abuse that her kids were suffering.

The end results were my mother's death, my dad's incarcerations, and my entry into foster care. Yes, I knew better. But the prospect of going into the deeper regions of my mind and seeing all the colors, and smelling all the smells, and thinking all the things I wouldn't allow myself to think in a normal state of mind felt too enticing to pass up.

The next week, I wanted to do it again. My school day had been all confusion. Thanksgiving was coming up and I couldn't convince my adoptive mom to cook, so I would be spending an uncomfortable Thanksgiving at someone else's house.

I felt alone and annoyed with everything, for no reason, or for reasons that I couldn't explain. I wanted a reprieve. But Caleb wasn't around. I

Drugs caused my mother's death, my dad's incarcerations, and my entry into foster care. Yes, I knew better.

didn't know what kind of over-the-counter cough medicine to take. So I called him from the nurse's office.

"Listen, I have a cold and want to take the medicine you gave me before. What's it called?"

He told me the brand and then added, "Only buy that one, and don't take more than 10."

I marched right out of school and went to the closest drug store and nervously bought the drug. I quickly left before my common sense could kick in and remind me of all the dangers of drug use, even technically legal drugs, which I knew could be just as addictive and destructive.

As soon as I got home I took eight. Then I waited. Nothing happened, so I figured it wasn't going to work. I called my friend, and she said that I should come over, that we were going out. So I went to my friend's house, feeling a tad disappointed that I wouldn't have the trip that I wanted, and that I had paid $6.09 for the damned things!

"Where are we going tonight?" I asked, laying back on my friend's bed.

"To church."

"What!" If there was one thing that I didn't need, it was a meeting with God.

"No, it's not like that. Me, you, Jylisha, and some other people are going to go to the Youth Service. It's going to be fun."

"Yeah, right," I thought.

I checked the clock: 6:00 maybe? I couldn't read it; it was spinning. Man, I was feeling woozy.

We left to gather the rest of our church-bound group. Lights seemed to be tiny suns orbiting street poles. Voices melded together and grew distant. My steps took an eternity and the air made me feel sick.

Like any addict, Caleb crossed the line from enjoying himself to damaging himself and he still didn't stop.

"I'm in too deep," I thought as the other members of our group joined us and I heard their names through the 10-foot tubes that my ears had become. I was afraid to cross the street. I wished I hadn't taken the pills.

At the church, I was afraid that everyone could tell that I was on drugs, and afraid the Big Brother in the Sky would see me and strike me with lightning. I was as quiet and distant as possible. I spoke only when asked directly, and only a few curt words. Everyone must have thought I was rude and weird.

"Are you feeling OK?" my best friend asked me with concern in her eyes.

All night I was spaced out. At one point, I went up and knelt down on the floor to be "saved by God." When I came back to where my friends were sitting, I asked how long I had been gone.

"Five minutes. Are you OK? You look a little funny," my friend said.

"I'm fine. I just had a religious experience. How would you look?" We smiled at my logic.

When we got home, I started spewing stuff straight off of crazy street: "No one can ever love me. My mother died because of me. I will never graduate. I'm a liar."

The next day, I felt guilty and told my friend what I'd done. "I'm gonna call a drug hotline for you," she said seriously. I felt so embarrassed.

That whole episode wasn't what I'd wanted or expected it to be. I had wanted a break from my crazy, worried, anxious, tired, bored state of mind. What I got was a restless and depressing night.

I was disappointed and discouraged. I started thinking of how much could've happened. I could have gotten physically hurt, or I could have hurt someone else or done something illegal. I realized that I am too afraid, and too scarred by my past, to ever feel that I'm above the consequences the way Caleb seemed to be.

The next time I saw Caleb it was all smiles and jokes. We were both sober—rare for him—and happy. He sat behind me in second period and we laughed with the rest of the class about the teacher we all hate. After class he told funny stories about Slovakia. "You're more fun when you're sober," I said.

On the bus I couldn't stop thinking about him. He seemed OK in life. He had a presumably happy family with both parents, and a girlfriend that he was in love with. When I asked, he said he was happy, that he just did drugs for fun.

It scared me to think that someone so apparently happy would do drugs so much. I felt sure there was something he wasn't telling me—something he wasn't telling himself.

Suddenly Caleb felt dangerous to me. He seemed like someone who rushed headfirst into danger with total disregard for the risks. I felt the consequences might yet come to him, and to me.

I thought, "Why am I drawn to Caleb? Is something wrong

with me? What if I don't turn out to be worthy or smart? What if I'm just a drug addict?" Later I convinced myself I was over-reacting.

A few weeks later, though, Caleb became concerned that he was having a psychotic break (losing touch with reality). He hadn't eaten much in days and was having hallucinations.

He looked up the symptoms associated with prolonged use of cold pills and found that he had some of them. He told me that he'd had a psychotic break before and it had lasted a couple of days, then went away. So he wasn't above the consequences. No one is.

I felt disappointed. I had hoped that Caleb would prove that not everyone ends up like the people in my family. And he hasn't: He wasn't behind bars, or running from the police. But his mind was paying a price.

Something changed for me after that. Caleb no longer seemed to have a happy, energetic light. I no longer believed that he used drugs just to have fun. I believed now that he was so far gone, so caught up in experiencing and experimenting, that he wouldn't stop taking drugs even when the stakes had become too high. Like any addict, he crossed the line from enjoying himself to damaging himself and he still didn't stop.

I haven't taken the pills since then. Sometimes I still want to turn into Not-Tasha, but my interest in drugs has faded a bit. I don't have the ache to try them like I did before. I've smoked weed a couple times, but that didn't feel like a great idea to me either.

I've come to realize that once you decide to deal with foreign substances, you sign a contract between you and the police, you and your body, and you and the universe to be out of control and to accept all consequences, including addiction.

If there's a time in my life when I feel curious again, or when I want to escape and get out of control, I'm going to be careful. I think it's best to try drugs—to try losing control—when you're feeling comfortable and good about yourself and what you're doing in life, not when you're feeling low and depressed. That seems like a recipe for addiction.

I still sometimes want to take some magic pill to disconnect from my life and my problems, at least briefly, or to inhale some mysterious plant that will allow me to feel uninhibited.

But I'm not going to do that now. I'll just have to come back down and deal with my problems. My little vacations could actually make my problems a lot worse. If I just deal with my life now, I might find a different way to let go.

Natasha was 19 when she wrote this story.
She went on to college.

Amir Soloman

Numbing Out the Past

By Miguel Ayala

It was lights out at the shelter. A few people were talking about sex and one person, Gigi, said she and her girl like to smoke weed, use heroin, or even settle on taking mad pills to feel happy before they have sex.

She said she took some cold pills from a drug store. "Once I did about 50 and chased it with a forty!" she said.

Like a jerk I said, "How does it feel?"

She rolled her eyes and said, "It makes you feel like your whole body is lead. You can't move. Everything is heavy. Your tongue is so heavy that when you talk, you drool!"

"That's hot," I thought. "I want to try it."

The first time I tried popping pills was a cool night. I was doing laundry at the laundromat. I had 10 tabs of cold medicine and Gigi and I split them two ways. We were talking and people were walking by as we waited for our clothes to dry. I was chain smoking. All of a sudden, BAM!

"Wait, be quiet, it just hit me!" I told Gigi. My body felt heavy and my brain felt slow, quiet, unworried, calm. I went home to the shelter, played some music, zoned out, and fell asleep.

The next day I felt relieved that I did not get caught coming in high and get kicked out of the shelter, but I also felt bad that I broke my sobriety. I'd been trying not to smoke weed or use any drugs.

For the next few days, any time I was mad I thought about pills. I remembered that D12 and Eminem song "Purple Pills" and its lyrics: "Blue and yellow purple pills!" After a couple of days being pissed off because I couldn't find any place to stay other than a shelter, I felt unable to calm down and started taking pills.

That was about six months ago. Ever since, I've been struggling with the temptation to use pills. For a while, I was popping pills every couple of days. Sometimes I'd take 24 tabs. I'd get a head-spinning sleepiness and the urge to throw up. I knew I was doing nothing but damage, but popping helped me forget the sorrow and the seemingly end-less pain I was feeling.

About a year ago I aged out of the foster care system, and since then I've been mostly homeless. Often I feel as if I am losing my mind and will never get it back.

I know I need to understand that I can't numb out pain with pills. There's got to be another way.

I'm also sad that I'll never have memories of being a little boy who was happy and safe at home. Pills, marijuana, and occasional drinking make it not hurt as much when I think about my family and being homeless.

When I think of my mom, I think of the moments when she showed me her love, her smiles. Then I remember one night when I was looking at a sunset from a window in my mother's home, and my family and I were playing cards for a quarter a hand. My mom was getting mad about losing money and started cussing in Spanish in a nasty tone.

She slammed her hands on the table and my mind rushed to the cold eye of the storm—times when my mom forced me to take off my clothes and lashed me with an extension cord on my face and chest. I'd put up an arm covered with welts and plead, "Stop, please, it hurts."

I'm willing to do almost anything to block out memories like that. When my mom directed her anger at me, I could not fight back. But now, when I get frustrated, I do what my mom did to me—I take the anger out on myself, harming myself by cutting or popping pills. Harming myself keeps me from hurting others, but it also hurts me. This year, I lost an apartment and my girlfriend because of pills.

I'm afraid of what's happening to me. I don't want to die like my pops—he OD'd on heroin—and leave people who care for me grieving. But I'm also not sure whether I can deal with my problems sober.

I realized that an apartment couldn't solve everything. It didn't get rid of my bad memories or stop me from feeling sad and alone.

A few months after I started popping pills, I finally found housing through a program for mentally ill people called Fountain House, where I also get therapy. The day I moved into my apartment, I felt like, "Yes! This homeless crap is over! I have my own crib and I can move on with my life."

But living by myself was also scary. I realized that an apartment couldn't solve everything. It didn't get rid of my bad memories or stop me from feeling sad and alone.

When I moved into the housing program, the agreement was that I would focus on my treatment and that I couldn't drink or use drugs. Whenever I felt like I wanted to harm myself, I had to take myself to the hospital. I broke all of those rules.

During that month, I got hospitalized several times after

popping pills. Then I took pills in front of a staff, and we had a meeting. The staff said, "You need to move out. What you did was very dangerous. You caused a lot of drama and endangered your life and the safety of yourself and everybody around you. And for that, you need to leave."

Soon I was upstairs packing.

From there I moved in with my girlfriend, Kenisha, who I'd known for almost three years. We first met at a Christmas party at Fountain House. She was wearing her hair all fancy and had on a nice outfit.

Living with Kenisha felt like walking on air at times, and walking on eggshells at others. She'd get pissed off at me but she could also be very loving.

One day I was writing about my past and I got so upset that I bought two bottles of pills, took five, and told my staff at Fountain House what I did. They told me that I needed to go to the hospital to deal with my feelings, and I did.

When Kenisha found out, she was furious. She was like a locomotive that wouldn't stop—fuming, steaming, and pissed off. She threw me out. The last thing she said to me was, "If you want to commit suicide, just do it."

Those nine words played in my head over and over like a broken record all night. Soon I was really thinking, "Just kill yourself, do the world a favor." I was also thinking, "I want to pop pills, pills, pills, pills!" Miraculously, I got through the night without popping. I slept on a table at a 24-hour Starbucks (and woke up stiff as hell!).

After that, I went back into shelters, and I'm still living in a shelter now. The shocking thing is that I haven't been popping pills at all. (I have been smoking a lot of weed.)

I wish I could find a drug that could get me really, really high without the mental fall-down that comes when I stop getting high. No, really, I just wish I could deal with this pain without doing something stupid to get by.

Not long ago, I saw my mom. When I got to her apartment, she was not there so I went to sleep in front of her door. I woke up about an hour later when she stepped off the elevator, looked at me and said, "Miguel, why are you sleeping on the floor? Stayed out all night, huh?"

I said, "No, my girl threw me out."

My mom asked, "What are you going to do?"

"I don't know…" I said, intentionally trailing off, hoping and praying she would say, "I have space here if you want to stay…" But she did not.

That afternoon, I slept on the couch for a few hours and ate. Then I went back to a shelter. I was so aggravated. All I could think was, "How could I go from a beautiful apartment to a shelter over something as stupid as pills?" I felt completely alone.

I know that popping pills will always push people away, not closer, but when I'm hurting, I don't know how to handle the pain. I don't know if I can stop hurting myself. Right now I'm dealing with too much. Nothing makes sense to me.

Life feels so cruel and unforgiving. I dream of a better life, without hurt or loneliness, where I don't have to suffer from my mental illness as much, and I can look forward to each and every new day with hope, not fear.

Sometimes I think I'll get there if I just say to myself, "Snap out of it!" I know I need to understand that I can't numb out pain with pills. There's got to be another way…I just don't know what that way is.

Miguel was 22 when he wrote this story. He has since found stable housing. And he no longer pops pills.

Jacob Reinstein

Busted!

By Anonymous

If you watch *Cops* on TV and you think you know what it's like to get arrested, let me tell you: That's not the half of it.

Last year, I got arrested for selling drugs, and when the cops came to the apartment where we were selling, oh man, that was scary. It was all happening so fast, I felt like my soul just left my body. I felt so numb, I forgot I was even standing.

It happened like this: I had been selling drugs for a few days with some other people in an old apartment. One day the cops started banging on the door. Then they busted it down and charged at everybody in the apartment.

They ran to the back room where I was. They grabbed me aggressively and smacked the cuffs on me hard. The cuffs weren't even on my wrists, but right above them, pressed down tight. When they loosened the cuffs later, you could see the marks where they cut into my arm.

Since I was in the back room by myself, I thought they were going to harm me or try to kill me since nobody was back there to know. They had me cuffed lying face down on the bed.

One of the cops had his knee on my back and his gun pressed to my head, so I didn't dare to so much as breathe the wrong way. One of the other cops yelled, "Don't @#$%-ing move!"

The one who had his gun to my head told me that I had every right to be scared, because if I didn't cooperate, he was seconds away from killing me, not with his gun, but with his bare hands.

Finally, they led me out of the apartment and brought me to the station, where they locked me in jail. I felt like an animal caged in. I had no privileges, no freedom.

Getting arrested was the most stressful thing I have ever gone through. Not only was it scary to get arrested, but I felt even worse that I disappointed a lot of people who found out, like my parents, my aunts, and my sister.

The cop who had his gun to my head told me that if I didn't cooperate, he would kill me.

When I called my parents, I felt ashamed to have to explain what happened. I didn't want them thinking that I was a bad kid. Their first reaction was, "What?!" and they were trying to bite my head off over the phone. My mother had a frying pan waiting for me to come home to.

My father was upset, but he didn't have very much to say. He just said, "I told you a million times about drugs," and, "You got what you deserve." His last words in that phone call were, "Watch your back while you're in jail."

They did not realize that I'd been having problems with money to the point where I decided to sell drugs. I needed the money because I was broke and didn't want to ask them for money. Plus my girl was pregnant, so I needed to pay for an abortion.

At the time, my family was getting on my case about finding

a job. They were tired of me being lazy and doing nothing. And when I asked them for money, they would be broke themselves from paying the bills.

I tried to get a job, but it was hard because I would fill out applications and go on interviews, but nobody would hire me. Maybe I gave up too easily, but I didn't know what to do, and dealing didn't seem so bad. It was fast money.

I was making hundreds of dollars a week. My ma grew suspicious about where I was getting the money, so I told her I had girls buying me stuff. I never thought I would end up in jail.

I spent two months in jail before my family was able to pay the bail. It was a big empty space with metal benches attached to the wall. There were other men in there with problems of their own, and I didn't really talk to them.

I had nothing to do all day but look at the walls or sleep. I kept thinking about what was going to happen to me when I went to see the judge, and if I was going to do hard time or not.

Spending that time in jail was even more stressful, scary, and shameful than getting arrested in the first place. I got through it by keeping my fingers crossed and praying.

I was hoping that they would dismiss my case, but it went on for a half a year, since it was a serious charge of possession of drugs—they had found 23 ounces of cocaine in the apartment. (I was lucky not to get charged for dealing. If the charge was dealing, then I would be doing time now.)

All my life growing up, my pa had told me about drugs: what they can do to you, how bad they are, and how selling or taking them is not the way to go.

In jail, I kept thinking to myself, "How did I get myself in this situation?" and I thought about how much I missed my family.

I could only imagine what kind of problems I was putting my poor mother through at home. And I knew how my father felt, because I could see it in his face the day they set my bail at $2,000 and sent me back through the system.

He was upset and hurt at the same time because he didn't want me going through that, and he was mad because I should have been smarter.

I felt like a big disappointment to myself and my family when I saw how helpless my father looked like that day. His face looked like he didn't know whether to cry or get mad. That ate me up inside.

I felt like a big disappointment when I saw how helpless my father looked like that day.

It seemed like my case went on forever. But finally, after six months, I just pleaded guilty and got five years probation. After it was over, I finally managed to get a job and make legal money. Now I go to see my probation officer once a month.

My parents still treat me how they treated me before, but I did have to earn my privileges back. They trust me now, but it took time for them to do that, too.

I would never sell drugs after all that, and I'm sure I never want to go to jail—and make my family feel so bad—again. So these days, I'm just staying out of trouble.

The writer was 19 and in high school
when he wrote this story.

Jamel Bloome

My Coke Phase

By Anonymous

It was Senior Day, one of the biggest parties of the year. At the party, my friend Frank gave me a hug and said, "Hold your hand out, I have a present for you." He put a hit of mescaline in my hand. Mesc is a hallucinogenic drug that looks like a tiny aspirin.

A lot of my friends had tripped before and said they had a lot of fun doing it, so I figured, why shouldn't I? I put it on my tongue, swallowed, and began my first trip.

I had a great time. I was seeing things completely differently; even colors were more vivid. And everything people said was so funny. I couldn't stop laughing. I was a lot more sociable that night than I usually am. I didn't feel shy at all. I met a lot of new people, including a girl named Kelly. I had heard a lot of stuff about how she and her sister Randi were crazy, and big druggies, but I liked her a lot.

A week later, my friend Pam and I met up with Kelly and the three of us went over to her house. We went upstairs to Randi's room and opened her door. She was standing over her desk with a razor blade in her hand. When she saw us, she smiled and told us to sit down. When I realized what she was doing, I was shocked. Randi was cutting up lines of cocaine. I didn't think I knew anyone who did coke.

I remember my eyes got really wide and I tried not to smile. I was wondering how doing coke would compare to my mescaline trip when Randi offered some to Pam and me. We immediately jumped at the chance.

I watched Randi do two lines and then I did exactly what she had done. I rolled up a dollar bill tightly, snorted a line, and jerked my head back. Then, I switched nostrils and went on to the next line. A couple of minutes later, I tasted something going down the back of my throat.

On cocaine, it seemed like everyone there really liked me.

A little while later, we went out again. We got on a bus to go to the beach. That's when I felt the coke hit me. I became very energetic. I was tapping my feet and biting my nails so much that Kelly had to tell me to stop because people were staring. Kelly thought that they would know we were high.

When we got to the beach, I was feeling really good. It seemed like everyone there really liked me. I felt confident and superior to them all. I was doing the same thing I did every other night, but it was so much more fun.

Nothing mattered except for the fact that I was having a great time and I never wanted it to end. But end it did—about an hour later. Even though it didn't last that long, I thought cocaine was the best high.

A couple of days later, I called Kelly and told her I wanted to do it again. I knew that she knew who the dealers were. I chipped in with her and we went down to the pool hall. We bought a small bag for $50 from two guys in their 20s.

We went back to Kelly's house and did half of it. I wanted to do the whole bag, but Kelly said we should save the rest for later, when we came down.

That's how it started. At first I was doing just three or four lines a week, usually before I went out with my friends or after I had a bad day. After a couple of weeks, I started doing two lines, three times a day (about half a gram).

The high I got from doing two lines would last about an hour. Pretty soon, even two lines wouldn't get me off anymore. I had to do at least four at a time to feel something. I started doing an eight-ball (about four grams) every four days.

The more I did, the higher I got, and I wanted to stay high for as long as possible. I was spending about $50 a week on coke and also getting a lot free from friends.

Summer vacation started. I would wake up at 2 p.m., shower, and go over to Kelly's. We'd eat dinner with her family, go down to the pool hall, and get a ride down to the beach. When we got there, we would break up lines with a credit card and snort. We'd sit on the beach around a fire with a bunch of other people who were screwed up in some way or another.

I started to mix drugs. Along with the coke, I would smoke pot, drink, and drop acid. I was so messed up every night, I couldn't even tell if the person who was driving was sober. I got into two really bad car accidents in a matter of three weeks. The police gave the drivers breathalyzer tests, but since they were tripping, not drunk, they passed.

My parents knew that I was smoking pot and that I had tripped a couple of times, but they thought it was just a phase I was going through, and that it would be over soon.

They didn't know I was doing coke and I didn't give them a chance to find out. I had stopped spending any time at all with my family, except for my younger sister. She would stay up to talk to me late at night and she knew I was screwed up. She told me I was a moron, but I really didn't care what she thought.

Then, one night, she started crying and told me that she hated me. She said, "I used to want to be just like you, but you're a stupid druggie." I was tripping when she said it. I tried to brush it off like it was nothing, but when I woke up to reality the next morning, it really upset me. I started crying and decided that I'd hide my drug use from her in the future.

Kelly's birthday was in August and I decided to have a big party for her at a park near my house. That night, I dropped three tabs of acid, smoked some weed, and did an eightball of coke. I normally would never do a whole eightball in eight hours, and I had never taken more than one and a half tabs of acid at once. I had really gone over my limit and I knew it.

I was supposed to be home by 1:30 a.m. I got in just in time and went into my mom's room and said "good night." Then I crawled out my bedroom window and went back to the party.

I came home again at 6 in the morning and found my mom waiting up for me. I had a really bad nosebleed when I walked in, and she saw the cocaine around my nostrils and the coke spoon on my neck. She started to cry. She asked me, "How can you even like it?"

I didn't really know what to say. We didn't argue. I just answered yes to everything she said. I actually thought the whole thing was funny at the time, but I kept a straight face, walked away, and went to sleep.

Later that day, me and my mom had a long talk. She was crying and asked me what other drugs I had done. I went through the list. Then she asked me how long I had been doing coke and how often. I told her the truth. She told me that she wanted me to go into rehab, but I convinced her that I'd straighten myself out.

At the time I didn't think I was addicted. I was just doing the drugs to be more sociable. If I wanted to stop, I didn't need any help doing it. And even if I did have a problem, who wants to sit around in a roomful of druggies listening to some shrink tell you what to do?

It still made me feel really bad watching my mom cry. I wanted to tell her that I was sorry, that I never meant to hurt her, that I didn't want to see her like that. But I didn't say any of those things. I didn't want to believe that my drug use was a problem for the people around me. I refused to admit that for a long time.

Instead, I promised my mom I would stop doing coke. I just didn't tell her when. There were still three weeks before school was going to start and I figured that once I was back in school I'd quit.

September came and I assumed everything would change. I was back in school and most of the people I had hung out with over the summer had gone away to college. But it wasn't that easy. First of all, everyone at school seemed to know I was using. Freshmen were coming up to me in the hall, asking if I had any weed they could buy. I asked a friend why this kept happening to me and he said people could tell by looking at me that I was screwed up.

At the time I didn't think I was addicted. I was just doing the drugs to be more sociable.

On top of that, school bored me. I went to every class, every day, for the first two weeks. But I didn't want to be there. I had no motivation or drive and I couldn't concentrate on what was going on in class. I was too busy trying to figure out where I could go to snort some coke.

I started spending less and less time at school. First I stopped going to gym. I decided that I was thin enough and didn't need to exercise. (Over the summer I had lost 35 pounds: The coke killed my appetite.) Next, I stopped going to English class.

Eventually, I just stopped going at all. I would wake up and get dressed and have my father drive me to school. Once he drove away, I'd get on a bus and go to my boyfriend's house. When I got there, I'd go back to sleep. When I woke up, we'd do some coke.

My parents couldn't figure out what was going on when they got my report card. My average for the previous term was a 93 and it had dropped to a 55. My mom flipped out. My dad just sat there and gave me dirty looks. He kept saying, "I'm very disappointed in you" and shaking his head.

They asked me if I was still doing all the drugs. I denied it because I was afraid they would try to make me go to a rehab center. I told them that I hated my school and I didn't want to go there anymore. My mom looked at my absences and said, "Obviously." We agreed that if I started doing better, I could change schools after the term was over.

But I continued to do really badly in school. I was doing coke before class, in the locker room, in the bathroom, whenever and wherever I could. Part of me was worried, because I wanted to get into a good college, far away, so I could move out of the house. But another part of me really couldn't care less.

For a while I even considered dropping out and getting my GED. Then I could go to a community college when I was ready. I talked to my dad about it and he got really mad. He had dropped out of school and never even got a GED. He told me that he was very lucky that he had a good, high-paying job and that in today's world, I would never be able to do what he did without a diploma. I stayed in school.

Meanwhile, my nosebleeds were getting more frequent. I was getting them all the time — at school, in the middle of the night, at parties. It happened about four times a week. Every time I touched my nose it felt really soft. I thought it was funny when I realized I was able to squish my nose flat into my face.

One day, my mother noticed the blood stains on my pillowcases. She asked what it was from. I couldn't come up with a good excuse, so I just stood there looking stupid.

My mom got absolutely furious. I'd never seen her so mad before. She grabbed my arm and dragged me to the car. She told me she was taking me to rehab. During the ride, I tried to get out of the car a few times, but couldn't. I begged and pleaded, but no matter what I said, she responded with, "I think I've heard that before." Finally I started crying. I think that's what convinced her to take me back home. I swore that I would quit, but I didn't.

By this point, even some of my friends seemed worried about me. They started coming up to me and asking me if I was off coke yet. I'd say yes, sure, whatever, shut up. But then my friend Dave, who I think of as a brother, sat me down to talk about it. We were in his basement and he was kind of drunk. He told me that he knew that I was still doing it. He looked at me so sincerely, and said, "I can't stand to see what you're doing to yourself." I really tried not to cry. He told me he loved me and would do anything he possibly could to help me get off it. I promised him I would and this time I really meant it.

I stayed in my house for the next couple of weeks. I went to school. I came home. I did my homework. I didn't buy any coke.

It was really hard. Twice, I went into convulsions because my body was going through withdrawal. I dreamed about doing coke and I wrote a story about how addicts never fully recover. I didn't know what to do with myself. My boyfriend and my friend Kelly were still doing a lot of drugs and the temptation was always there.

I swore that I would quit, but I didn't.

It's been a little over a year now since I stopped doing drugs but there are reminders everywhere. The bridge of my nose is still somewhat soft: I think it's healed as much as it's going to. I have a very short attention span now. I lose my train of thought constantly and get bored quickly. School used to be easy for me but now I have trouble concentrating. My grades have dropped and when I took the SAT I got so aggravated that I just rushed through it. In short, I'm burnt.

If I hadn't stopped when I did, I'd probably be in even worse shape. I would have become a potato, like some people I know who do nothing but sit and watch TV and go, "Wow, man." Then there's the friend of a friend who mixed heroin and coke and died. That could have happened to me.

I guess that if it wasn't for Dave, I might still be snorting my life away. What he said to me really hit home. Maybe it didn't sink in when my parents tried to talk to me because they're authority figures and I didn't want them telling me what to do. But when a friend who means the world to you decides to say something, it really makes you think. "Dave wants me to have a good time, but not this way," I said to myself. "It's wrong."

I never thanked Dave with words, but I hope he realizes that I would do anything to repay him. If he didn't before, he will now.

The author was in high school when she wrote this story.

YC Art Dept.

Getting Help

Thinking about getting help? You've got a lot of options. Here are some of the different kinds of drug treatment available:

• **Detoxification** (detox) programs help men and women addicted to alcohol or drugs to go through the withdrawal process under the supervision of a medical professional. The length of time you stay depends on the drug—it could be two days or two weeks. In many detox programs medication is prescribed to ease the symptoms of withdrawal.

Detoxification alone is not enough for most people to maintain a sober, healthy lifestyle—detox should be accompanied by or followed by outpatient or inpatient treatment

• **Inpatient / Residential programs** can be short- or long-term. Short-term programs are generally 21 or 28 days. Long term programs can last for up to two years. Treatment may be in a hospital or an independent facility, and the doors may be locked or unlocked.

• **Therapeutic community treatment** is inpatient treatment based on the concept of mutual self-help: residents take an active part in their recovery, and accept the support and sanctions of their peers.

• **Outpatient programs** offer emergency help, evaluation and referral services, and short-term treatment for clients who are living at home.

• **12-step programs** are ongoing, anonymous, self-help group meetings for people with similar problems (e.g. Alcoholics Anonymous) who get together to talk about their experiences, hopes, challenges and next steps.

• **Counseling** for individuals, groups, or families can help both addicts and their friends and families.

No matter what kind of treatment you try, there is more to recovery than quitting drugs. Effective treatment works on many aspects of a person's life: self-esteem, family relationships and friendships, learning problems, criminal behavior, and more.

In order to stay clean, addicts need to examine their past, and identify triggers that may lead them back to substance abuse. Patients in treatment are asked to identify people, places, and things that they associate with their addiction.

Reprinted with permission from phoenixhouse.org

For Further Information

If you want to do more exploration on your own, take a look at these websites. They have reliable, teen-friendly information about drug use, addiction, and how you can get help.

Phoenix House
http://www.phoenixhouse.org/
Phoenix House is a non-profit drug and alcohol treatment and prevention program operating in California, New York, New England, Florida, and Texas. It also has an extensive section of online resources and reliable information to get you started with finding help—wherever you live.

National Institute on Drug Abuse for Teens
http://teens.drugabuse.gov/
On this government website, you can view frequently asked questions (FAQs) and fact sheets about addiction and the effects of specific drugs.

Partnership for a Drug-Free America
http://www.drugfree.org/
This site has a teen section featuring FAQs, fact sheets, personal stories, and a bulletin board to post your comments. There's also a treatment section, where you can find contact information for treatment programs and hotlines nationwide.

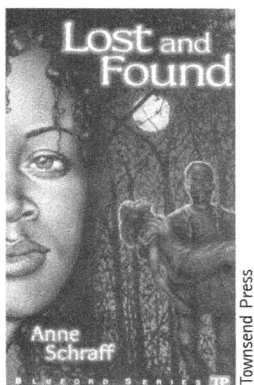
Townsend Press

Lost and Found

Darcy Wills winced at the loud rap music coming from her sister's room.

My rhymes were rockin'
MC's were droppin'
People shoutin' and hip-hoppin'
Step to me and you'll be inferior
'Cause I'm your lyrical superior.

Darcy went to Grandma's room. The darkened room smelled of lilac perfume, Grandma's favorite, but since her stroke Grandma did not notice it, or much of anything.

"Bye, Grandma," Darcy whispered from the doorway. "I'm going to school now."

Just then, the music from Jamee's room cut off, and Jamee rushed into the hallway.

The teen characters in the Bluford novels, a fiction series by Townsend Press, struggle with many of the same difficult issues as the writers in this book. Here's the first chapter from *Lost and Found*, by Anne Schraff, the first book in the series. In this novel, high school sophomore Darcy contends with the return of her long-absent father, the troubling behavior of her younger sister Jamee, and the beginning of her first relationship.

"Like she even hears you," Jamee said as she passed Darcy. Just two years younger than Darcy, Jamee was in eighth grade, though she looked older.

"It's still nice to talk to her. Sometimes she understands. You want to pretend she's not here or something?"

"She's not," Jamee said, grabbing her backpack.

"Did you study for your math test?" Darcy asked. Mom was an emergency room nurse who worked rotating shifts. Most of the time, Mom was too tired to pay much attention to the girls' schoolwork. So Darcy tried to keep track of Jamee.

"Mind your own business," Jamee snapped.

"You got two D's on your last report card," Darcy scolded. "You wanna flunk?" Darcy did not want to sound like a nagging parent, but Jamee wasn't doing her best. Maybe she couldn't make A's like Darcy, but she could do better.

Jamee stomped out of the apartment, slamming the door behind her. "Mom's trying to get some rest!" Darcy yelled. "Do you have to be so selfish?" But Jamee was already gone, and the apartment was suddenly quiet.

Darcy loved her sister. Once, they had been good friends. But now all Jamee cared about was her new group of rowdy friends. They leaned on cars outside of school and turned up rap music on their boom boxes until the street seemed to tremble like an earthquake. Jamee had even stopped hanging out with her old friend Alisha Wrobel, something she used to do every weekend.

Darcy went back into the living room, where her mother sat in the recliner sipping coffee. "I'll be home at 2:30, Mom," Darcy said. Mom smiled faintly. She was tired, always tired. And lately she was worried too. The hospital where she worked was cutting staff. It seemed each day fewer people were expected to do more work. It was like trying to climb a mountain that keeps getting taller as you go. Mom was forty-four, but just yesterday she said, "I'm like an old car that's run out of warranty, baby. You know what happens then. Old car is ready for the junk heap. Well, maybe that hospital is gonna tell me one of these days—'Mattie Mae Wills, we don't need you anymore. We can get somebody younger and cheaper.'"

"Mom, you're not old at all," Darcy had said, but they were only words, empty words. They could not erase the dark, weary lines from beneath her mother's eyes.

Darcy headed down the street toward Bluford High School. It was not a terrible neighborhood they lived in; it just was not good. Many front yards were not cared for. Debris—fast food wrappers, plastic bags, old newspapers—blew around and piled against fences and curbs. Darcy hated that. Sometimes she and other kids from school spent Saturday mornings cleaning up, but it seemed a losing battle. Now, as she walked, she tried to focus on small spots of beauty along the way. Mrs. Walker's pink and white roses bobbed proudly in the morning breeze. The Hustons' rock garden was carefully designed around a wooden windmill.

As she neared Bluford, Darcy thought about the science project that her biology teacher, Ms. Reed, was assigning. Darcy was doing hers on tidal pools. She was looking forward to visiting a real tidal pool, taking pictures, and doing research. Today, Ms. Reed would be dividing the students into teams of two. Darcy wanted to be paired with her close friend, Brisana Meeks. They were both excellent students, a cut above most kids at Bluford, Darcy thought.

"Today, we are forming project teams so that each student can gain something valuable from the other," Ms. Reed said as Darcy sat at her desk. Ms. Reed was a tall, stately woman who reminded Darcy of the Statue of Liberty. She would have been a perfect model for the statue if Lady Liberty had been a black woman. She never would have been called pretty, but it was possible she might have been called a handsome woman. "For this assignment, each of you will be working with someone you've never worked with before."

Darcy was worried. If she was not teamed with Brisana,

maybe she would be teamed with some really dumb student who would pull her down. Darcy was a little ashamed of herself for thinking that way. Grandma used to say that all flowers are equal, but different. The simple daisy was just as lovely as the prize rose. But still Darcy did not want to be paired with some weak partner who would lower her grade.

"Darcy Wills will be teamed with Tarah Carson," Ms. Reed announced.

Darcy gasped. Not Tarah! Not that big, chunky girl with the brassy voice who squeezed herself into tight skirts and wore lime green or hot pink satin tops and cheap jewelry. Not Tarah who hung out with Cooper Hodden, that loser who was barely hanging on to his football eligibility. Darcy had heard that Cooper had been left back once or twice and even got his driver's license as a sophomore. Darcy's face felt hot with anger. Why was Ms. Reed doing this?

Hakeem Randall, a handsome, shy boy who sat in the back row, was teamed with the class blabbermouth, LaShawn Appleby. Darcy had a secret crush on Hakeem since freshman year. So far she had only shared this with her diary, never with another living soul.

It was almost as though Ms. Reed was playing some devilish game. Darcy glanced at Tarah, who was smiling broadly. Tarah had an enormous smile, and her teeth contrasted harshly with her dark red lipstick. "Great," Darcy muttered under her breath.

Ms. Reed ordered the teams to meet so they could begin to plan their projects.

As she sat down by Tarah, Darcy was instantly sickened by a syrupy-sweet odor.

She must have doused herself with cheap perfume this morning , Darcy thought.

"Hey, girl," Tarah said. "Well, don't you look down in the mouth. What's got you lookin' that way?"

It was hard for Darcy to meet new people, especially someone like Tarah, a person Aunt Charlotte would call "low class." These were people who were loud and rude. They drank too much, used drugs, got into fights and ruined the neighborhood. They yelled ugly insults at people, even at their friends. Darcy did not actually know that Tarah did anything like this personally, but she seemed like the type who did.

"I just didn't think you'd be interested in tidal pools," Darcy explained.

Tarah slammed her big hand on the desk, making her gold bracelets jangle like ice cubes in a glass, and laughed. Darcy had never heard a mule bray, but she was sure it made exactly the same sound. Then Tarah leaned close and whispered, "Girl, I don't know a tidal pool from a fool. Ms. Reed stuck us together to mess with our heads, you hear what I'm sayin'?"

"Maybe we could switch to other partners," Darcy said nervously.

A big smile spread slowly over Tarah's face. "Nah, I think I'm gonna enjoy this. You're always sittin' here like a princess collecting your A's. Now you gotta work with a regular person, so you better loosen up, girl!"

Darcy felt as if her teeth were glued to her tongue. She fumbled in her bag for her outline of the project. It all seemed like a horrible joke now. She and Tarah Carson standing knee-deep in the muck of a tidal pool!

"Worms live there, don't they?" Tarah asked, twisting a big gold ring on her chubby finger.

"Yeah, I guess," Darcy replied.

"Big green worms," Tarah continued. "So if you get your feet stuck in the bottom of that old tidal pool, and you can't get out, do the worms crawl up your clothes?"

Darcy ignored the remark. "I'd like for us to go there soon, you know, look around."

"My boyfriend, Cooper, he goes down to the ocean all the time. He can take us. He says he's seen these fiddler crabs. They look like big spiders, and they'll try to bite your toes off. Cooper says so," Tarah said.

"Stop being silly," Darcy shot back. "If you're not even going to be serious . . . "

"You think you're better than me, don't you?" Tarah suddenly growled.

"I never said—" Darcy blurted.

"You don't have to say it, girl. It's in your eyes. You think I'm a low-life and you're something special. Well, I got more friends than you got fingers and toes together. You got no friends, and everybody laughs at you behind your back. Know what the word on you is? Darcy Wills give you the chills."

Just then, the bell rang, and Darcy was glad for the excuse to turn away from Tarah, to hide the hot tears welling in her eyes. She quickly rushed from the classroom, relieved that school was over. Darcy did not think she could bear to sit through another class just now.

Darcy headed down the long street towards home. She did not like Tarah. Maybe it was wrong, but it was true. Still, Tarah's brutal words hurt. Even stupid, awful people might tell you the truth about yourself. And Darcy did not have any real friends, except for Brisana. Maybe the other kids were mocking her behind her back. Darcy was very slender, not as shapely as many of the other girls. She remembered the time when Cooper Hodden was hanging in front of the deli with his friends, and he yelled as Darcy went by, "Hey, is that really a female there? Sure don't look like it. Looks more like an old broomstick with hair. " His companions laughed rudely, and Darcy had walked a little faster.

A terrible thought clawed at Darcy. Maybe she was the loser, not Tarah. Tarah was always hanging with a bunch of kids, laughing and joking. She would go down the hall to the lockers and greetings would come from everywhere. "Hey, Tarah!" "What's up, Tar?" "See ya at lunch, girl." When Darcy went to the lockers, there was dead silence.

Darcy usually glanced into stores on her way home from school. She enjoyed looking at the trays of chicken feet and pork ears at the little Asian grocery store. Sometimes she would even steal a glance at the diners sitting by the picture window at the Golden Grill Restaurant. But today she stared straight ahead, her shoulders drooping.

If this had happened last year, she would have gone directly to Grandma's house, a block from where Darcy lived. How many times had Darcy and Jamee run to Grandma's, eaten applesauce cookies, drunk cider, and poured out their troubles to Grandma. Somehow, their problems would always dissolve in the warmth of her love and wisdom. But now Grandma was a frail figure in the corner of their apartment, saying little. And what little she did say made less and less sense.

Darcy was usually the first one home. The minute she got there, Mom left for the hospital to take the 3:00 to 11:00 shift in the ER. By the time Mom finished her paperwork at the hospital, she would be lucky to be home again by midnight. After Mom left, Darcy went to Grandma's room to give her the malted nutrition drink that the doctor ordered her to have three times a day.

"Want to drink your chocolate malt, Grandma?" Darcy asked, pulling up a chair beside Grandma's bed.

Grandma was sitting up, and her eyes were open. "No. I'm not hungry," she said listlessly. She always said that.

"You need to drink your malt, Grandma," Darcy insisted, gently putting the straw between the pinched lips.

Grandma sucked the malt slowly. "Grandma, nobody likes me at school," Darcy said. She did not expect any response. But there was a strange comfort in telling Grandma anyway. "Everybody laughs at me. It's because I'm shy and maybe stuck-up, too, I guess. But I don't mean to be. Stuck-up, I mean. Maybe I'm weird. I could be weird, I guess. I could be like Aunt Charlotte . . ." Tears rolled down Darcy's cheeks. Her heart ached with loneliness. There was nobody to talk to anymore, nobody who had time to listen, nobody who understood.

Grandma blinked and pushed the straw away. Her eyes brightened as they did now and then. "You are a wonderful girl. Everybody knows that," Grandma said in an almost normal voice. It happened like that sometimes. It was like being in the middle of a dark storm and having the clouds part, revealing a patch of clear, sunlit blue. For just a few precious minutes, Grandma was bright-eyed and saying normal things.

"Oh, Grandma, I'm so lonely," Darcy cried, pressing her head against Grandma's small shoulder.

"You were such a beautiful baby," Grandma said, stroking her hair. "'That one is going to shine like the morning star.' That's what I told your Mama. 'That child is going to shine like the morning star.' Tell me, Angelcake, is your daddy home yet?"

Darcy straightened. "Not yet." Her heart pounded so hard, she could feel it thumping in her chest. Darcy's father had not been home in five years.

"Well, tell him to see me when he gets home. I want him to buy you that blue dress you liked in the store window. That's for you, Angelcake. Tell him I've got money. My social security came, you know. I have money for the blue dress," Grandma said, her eyes slipping shut.

Just then, Darcy heard the apartment door slam. Jamee had come home. Now she stood in the hall, her hands belligerently on her hips. "Are you talking to Grandma again?" Jamee demanded.

"She was talking like normal," Darcy said. "Sometimes she does. You know she does."

"That is so stupid," Jamee snapped. "She never says anything right anymore. Not anything!" Jamee's voice trembled.

Darcy got up quickly and set down the can of malted milk. She ran to Jamee and put her arms around her sister. "Jamee, I know you're hurting too."

"Oh, don't be stupid," Jamee protested, but Darcy hugged her more tightly, and in a few seconds Jamee was crying. "She was the best thing in this stupid house," Jamee cried. "Why'd she have to go?"

"She didn't go," Darcy said. "Not really."

"She did! She did!" Jamee sobbed. She struggled free of Darcy, ran to her room, and slammed the door. In a minute, Darcy heard the bone-rattling sound of rap music.

Lost and Found, a Bluford Series™ novel, is reprinted with permission from Townsend Press. Copyright © 2002.

Want to read more? This and other Bluford Series™ novels and paperbacks can be purchased for $1 each at www.townsendpress.com.

Teens:
How to Get More Out of This Book

Self-help: The teens who wrote the stories in this book did so because they hope that telling their stories will help readers who are facing similar challenges. They want you to know that you are not alone, and that taking specific steps can help you manage or overcome very difficult situations. They've done their best to be clear about the actions that worked for them so you can see if they'll work for you.

Writing: You can also use the book to improve your writing skills. Each teen in this book wrote 5-10 drafts of his or her story before it was published. If you read the stories closely you'll see that the teens work to include a beginning, a middle, and an end, and good scenes, description, dialogue, and anecdotes (little stories). To improve your writing, take a look at how these writers construct their stories. Try some of their techniques in your own writing.

Reading: Finally, you'll notice that we include the first chapter from a Bluford Series novel in this book, alongside the true stories by teens. We hope you'll like it enough to continue reading. The more you read, the more you'll strengthen your reading skills. Teens at Youth Communication like the Bluford novels because they explore themes similar to those in their own stories. Your school may already have the Bluford books. If not, you can order them online for only $1.

Resources on the Web

We will occasionally post Think About It questions on our website, www.youthcomm.org, to accompany stories in this and other Youth Communication books. We try out the questions with teens and post the ones they like best. Many teens report that writing answers to those questions in a journal is very helpful.

How to Use This Book in Staff Training

Staff say that reading these stories gives them greater insight into what teens are thinking and feeling, and new strategies for working with them. You can help the staff you work with by using these stories as case studies.

Select one story to read in the group, and ask staff to identify and discuss the main issue facing the teen. There may be disagreement about this, based on the background and experience of staff. That is fine. One point of the exercise is that teens have complex lives and needs. Adults can probably be more effective if they don't focus too narrowly and can see several dimensions of their clients.

Ask staff: What issues or feelings does the story provoke in them? What kind of help do they think the teen wants? What interventions are likely to be most promising? Least effective? Why? How would you build trust with the teen writer? How have other adults failed the teen, and how might that affect his or her willingness to accept help? What other resources would be helpful to this teen, such as peer support, a mentor, counseling, family therapy, etc?

Resources on the Web

From time to time we will post Think About It questions on our website, www.youthcomm.org, to accompany stories in this and other Youth Communication books. We try out the questions with teens and post the ones that they find most effective. We'll also post lessons for some of the stories. Adults can use the questions and lessons in workshops.

Teachers and Staff:
How to Use This Book in Groups

When working with teens individually or in groups, you can use these stories to help young people face difficult issues in a way that feels safe to them. That's because talking about the issues in the stories usually feels safer to teens than talking about those same issues in their own lives. Addressing issues through the stories allows for some personal distance; they hit close to home, but not too close. Talking about them opens up a safe place for reflection. As teens gain confidence talking about the issues in the stories, they usually become more comfortable talking about those issues in their own lives.

Below are general questions to guide your discussion. In most cases you can read a story and conduct a discussion in one 45-minute session. Teens are usually happy to read the stories aloud, with each teen reading a paragraph or two. (Allow teens to pass if they don't want to read.) It takes 10-15 minutes to read a story straight through. However, it is often more effective to let workshop participants make comments and discuss the story as you go along. The workshop leader may even want to annotate her copy of the story beforehand with key questions.

If teens read the story ahead of time or silently, it's good to break the ice with a few questions that get everyone on the same page: Who is the main character? How old is she? What happened to her? How did she respond? Another good starting question is: "What stood out for you in the story?" Go around the room and let each person briefly mention one thing.

Then move on to open-ended questions, which encourage participants to think more deeply about what the writers were feeling, the choices they faced, and the actions they took. There are no right or wrong answers to the open-ended questions.

Open-ended questions encourage participants to think about how the themes, emotions, and choices in the stories relate to their own lives. Here are some examples of open-ended questions that we have found to be effective. You can use variations of these questions with almost any story in this book.

—What main problem or challenge did the writer face?

—What choices did the teen have in trying to deal with the problem?

—Which way of dealing with the problem was most effective for the teen? Why?

—What strengths, skills, or resources did the teen use to address the challenge?

—If you were in the writer's shoes, what would you have done?

—What could adults have done better to help this young person?

—What have you learned by reading this story that you didn't know before?

—What, if anything, will you do differently after reading this story?

—What surprised you in this story?

—Do you have a different view of this issue, or see a different way of dealing with it, after reading this story? Why or why not?

Credits

The stories in this book originally appeared in the following
Youth Communication publications:

"Clean and Kind of Sober," by Antwaun Garcia, *Represent*, May/June 2005; "Last Man Standing," by Russell Morse, *Represent*, September/October 2000; "Hooked on Heroin," by Anonymous, *Represent*, January/February 2003; "My Battle to Quit," by Ashunte Hunt, *Represent*, November/December 2007; "What Drugs Do to You (Even the Legal Ones)," *New Youth Connections*, December 2007; "Ecstasy Proved to Be Anything But," by M. Lopez, *Represent*, May/June 2005; "Becoming Someone Else," by Daniel Verzhbo, *Represent*, January/February 2008; "Losing My Life to Drugs," by Anonymous, *New Youth Connections*, November 2001; "My REAL Reasons for Quitting Weed," by X. Reyes, *Represent*, July/August 1994; "Interviews with Dealers: Taking Care of Business?" by Anonymous, *Represent*, January/February 1999; "My So-Called Holidays," by Sidney Black, *Represent*, March/April 2000; "Smoke and Mirrors," by Anonymous, *Represent*, July/August 2003; "How to Get to LaLa Land," by Anonymous, *Represent*, September/ October 2000; "If You Trip, You Might Fall," by Anonymous, *New Youth Connections*, May/June 1996; "A Fine Line Between Experimentation and Addiction," by Natasha Santos, *Represent*, March/April 2004; "Numbing Out the Past," by Miguel Ayala, *Represent*, May/June 2005; "Busted!" by Anonymous, *Represent*, January/February 2004; "My Coke Phase," by Anonymous, *New Youth Connections*, December 1992; "Getting Help," *New Youth Connections*, December 2007.

About
Youth Communication

Youth Communication, founded in 1980, is a nonprofit youth development program located in New York City whose mission is to teach writing, journalism, and leadership skills. The teenagers we train become writers for our websites and books and for two print magazines: *New Youth Connections*, a general-interest youth magazine, and *Represent*, a magazine by and for young people in foster care.

Each year, up to 100 young people participate in Youth Communication's school-year and summer journalism workshops, where they work under the direction of full-time professional editors. Most are African-American, Latino, or Asian, and many are recent immigrants. The opportunity to reach their peers with accurate portrayals of their lives and important self-help information motivates the young writers to create powerful stories.

Our goal is to run a strong youth development program in which teens produce high quality stories that inform and inspire their peers. Doing so requires us to be sensitive to the complicated lives and emotions of the teen participants while also providing an intellectually rigorous experience. We achieve that goal in the writing/teaching/editing relationship, which is the core of our program.

Our teaching and editorial process begins with discussions

between adult editors and the teen staff. In those meetings, the teens and the editors work together to identify the most important issues in the teens' lives and to figure out how those issues can be turned into stories that will resonate with teen readers.

Once story topics are chosen, students begin the process of crafting their stories. For a personal story, that means revisiting events in one's past to understand their significance for the future. For a commentary, it means developing a logical and persuasive point of view. For a reported story, it means gathering information through research and interviews. Students look inward and outward as they try to make sense of their experiences and the world around them and find the points of intersection between personal and social concerns. That process can take a few weeks or a few months. Stories frequently go through ten or more drafts as students work under the guidance of their editors, the way any professional writer does.

Many of the students who walk through our doors have uneven skills, as a result of poor education, living under extremely stressful conditions, or coming from homes where English is a second language. Yet, to complete their stories, students must successfully perform a wide range of activities, including writing and rewriting, reading, discussion, reflection, research, interviewing, and typing. They must work as members of a team and they must accept individual responsibility. They learn to provide constructive criticism, and to accept it. They engage in explorations of truthfulness, fairness, and accuracy. They meet deadlines. They must develop the audacity to believe that they have something important to say and the humility to recognize that saying it well is not a process of instant gratification. Rather, it usually requires a long, hard struggle through many discussions and much rewriting.

It would be impossible to teach these skills and dispositions as separate, disconnected topics, like grammar, ethics, or assertiveness. However, we find that students make rapid progress when they are learning skills in the context of an inquiry that is personally significant to them and that will benefit their peers.

When teens publish their stories—in *New Youth Connections* and *Represent*, on the web, and in other publications—they reach tens of thousands of teen and adult readers. Teachers, counselors, social workers, and other adults circulate the stories to young people in their classes and out-of-school youth programs. Adults tell us that teens in their programs—including many who are ordinarily resistant to reading—clamor for the stories. Teen readers report that the stories give them information they can't get anywhere else, and inspire them to reflect on their lives and open lines of communication with adults.

Writers usually participate in our program for one semester, though some stay much longer. Years later, many of them report that working here was a turning point in their lives—that it helped them acquire the confidence and skills that they needed for success in college and careers. Scores of our graduates have overcome tremendous obstacles to become journalists, writers, and novelists. They include National Book Award finalist and MacArthur Fellowship winner Edwidge Danticat, novelist Ernesto Quiñonez, writer Veronica Chambers, and *New York Times* reporter Rachel Swarns. Hundreds more are working in law, business, and other careers. Many are teachers, principals, and youth workers, and several have started nonprofit youth programs themselves and work as mentors—helping another generation of young people develop their skills and find their voices.

Youth Communication is a nonprofit educational corporation. Contributions are gratefully accepted and are tax deductible to the fullest extent of the law.

To make a contribution, or for information about our publications and programs, including our catalog of over 100 books and curricula for hard-to-reach teens, see www.youthcomm.org

About the Editors

Virginia Vitzthum is an editor at *Represent*, Youth Communication's magazine by and for teens in foster care. Before working at Youth Communication she wrote a book about Internet dating and a column for the web magazine salon.com. She's also written for *Ms., Elle, the Village Voice, Time Out New York, Washington City Paper*, and other publications. She has edited law books as well as books about substance abuse treatment and health care policy newsletters. She's written a play and a screenplay; produced several short videos; and volunteered at the 52nd St. Project, a children's theater, where she helped 9- to 11-year-olds write plays.

Keith Hefner co-founded Youth Communication in 1980 and has directed it ever since. He is the recipient of the Luther P. Jackson Education Award from the New York Association of Black Journalists and a MacArthur Fellowship. He was also a Revson Fellow at Columbia University.

Laura Longhine is the editorial director at Youth Communication. She edited *Represent*, Youth Communication's magazine by and for youth in foster care, for three years, and has written for a variety of publications. She has a BA in English from Tufts University and an MS in Journalism from Columbia University.

More Helpful Books
From Youth Comunication

The Struggle to Be Strong: True Stories by Teens About Overcoming Tough Times. Foreword by Veronica Chambers. Help young people identify and build on their own strengths with 30 personal stories about resiliency. (Free Spirit)

Starting With "I": Personal Stories by Teenagers. "Who am I and who do I want to become?" Thirty-five stories examine this question through the lens of race, ethnicity, gender, sexuality, family, and more. Increase this book's value with the free Teacher's Guide, available from youthcomm.org. (Youth Communication)

Real Stories, Real Teens. Inspire teens to read and recognize their strengths with this collection of 26 true stories by teens. The young writers describe how they overcame significant challenges and stayed true to themselves. Also includes the first chapters from three novels in the Bluford Series. (Youth Communication)

The Courage to Be Yourself: True Stories by Teens About Cliques, Conflicts, and Overcoming Peer Pressure. In 26 first-person stories, teens write about their lives with searing honesty. These stories will inspire young readers to reflect on their own lives, work through their problems, and help them discover who they really are. (Free Spirit)

Out With It: Gay and Straight Teens Write About Homosexuality. Break stereotypes and provide support with this unflinching look at gay life from a teen's perspective. With a focus on urban youth, this book also includes several heterosexual teens' transformative experiences with gay peers. (Youth Communication)

Things Get Hectic: Teens Write About the Violence That Surrounds Them. Violence is commonplace in many teens' lives, be it bullying, gangs, dating, or family relationships. Hear the experiences of victims, perpetrators, and witnesses through more than 50 real-world stories. (Youth Communication)

From Dropout to Achiever: Teens Write About School. Help teens overcome the challenges of graduating, which may involve overcoming family problems, bouncing back from a bad semester, or even dropping out for a time. These teens show how they achieve academic success. (Youth Communication)

My Secret Addiction: Teens Write About Cutting. These true accounts of cutting, or self-mutilation, offer a window into the personal and family situations that lead to this secret habit, and show how teens can get the help they need. (Youth Communication)

Sticks and Stones: Teens Write About Bullying. Shed light on bullying, as told from the perspectives of the bully, the victim, and the witness. These stories show why bullying occurs, the harm it causes, and how it might be prevented. (Youth Communication)

Boys to Men: Teens Write About Becoming a Man. The young men in this book write about confronting the challenges of growing up. Their honesty and courage make them role models for teens who are bombarded with contradictory messages about what it means to be a man. (Youth Communication)

Watching My Parents Disappear: Teens Write About Addiction in the Family. Dealing with a parent who has an addiction can be emotionally overwhelming and even dangerous. The true stories in this book will inspire teens in similar situations to seek support, and remind them that a parent's addiction is not their responsibility, and not their fault. (Youth Communication)

To order these and other books, go to:
www.youthcomm.org
or call 212-279-0708 x115

www.ingramcontent.com/pod-product-compliance
Lightning Source LLC
Chambersburg PA
CBHW051725090426
42738CB00010B/2087